THE GAZA TRIBUNAL

'An extraordinary act of truth-telling and accountability for one of the greatest crimes of our time. This book is essential in the pursuit of justice for the Palestinian people, and an example for people around the world seeking to hold their governments to account for complicity in genocide.'

—FRANCESCA ALBANESE,
UN Special Rapporteur on the Occupied Palestinian Territories

'We have learnt that "genocide denial" is a critical part of any genocidal project. The Gaza Tribunal is part of our resistance to the genocide, its enablement and its denial.'

—DR GHASSAN ABU SITTAH,
award-winning surgeon, activist and educator

'At a time of criminalisation and demonisation of pro-Palestinian activism, the Gaza Tribunal establishes who the real law-breakers are. Scrupulously applying international humanitarian law, this book demonstrates, clearly, convincingly and devastatingly, that two successive British governments have not only been complicit but participant in genocide.'

—NORMAN FINKELSTEIN,
author of *Gaza* and *The Holocaust Industry*,
and DEBORAH MACCOBY,
Jewish Voice for Liberation

'The total destruction of Gaza's healthcare system and the systematic targeting of doctors, nurses, paramedics and hospitals will remain one of the defining moral crimes of our era.

The Gaza Tribunal is a vital act of resistance against genocide, medicide and their denial — preserving truth for the historical record and bearing witness to the extraordinary courage of Palestinian health workers who continued to save lives under unimaginable conditions.'

—DR. OMAR ABDEL-MANNAN,
co-founder of Health Workers 4 Palestine

'Operating on a shoestring and without true access to the people that took decisions inside the UK government, the Gaza Tribunal, over two often riveting days, asked the questions about what happened in Gaza and UK complicity that parliament unfortunately failed to ask.'

—PATRICK WINTOUR,
journalist, diplomatic editor for the *Guardian*

'More than any other country, the United Kingdom bears a profound and enduring responsibility for the decades-long oppression of the Palestinian people. The Gaza Tribunal weaves frontline testimonies with sharp political and historical analysis to expose Britain's complicity in Israel's war crimes and its genocide of the Palestinian people. It stands as an unyielding record of the on-the-ground reality and an urgent demand for absolute accountability from the government, institutions and individuals involved.'

—MOSAB ABU TOHA,
author of *Forest of Noise*

'The genocide in Gaza may well be one of the defining moments of our era. It is certainly one of the most horrific. This book is an important one, not least because it does what all the

Western and other allies of Israel were unwilling to do, which is apply the fundamental tenets of international law to Israel. It is a fascinating, horrifying account and an important book for anyone who cares about human rights or human decency.'

—DIANE ABBOTT MP

'This report is sober, scrupulous, quietly devastating and of first-class importance.'

—PETER OBORNE,
journalist and broadcaster

'We are living through a time of destruction featuring the complicity of governments and the relentless protest of ordinary people. The Gaza Tribunal in Britain is one brilliant example of how people moved with agency, insisted on accountability and honored the dignity of the Palestinian people who have refused to surrender. This book adds to an archive that rightly called genocide by its name and made real the commitment, never again, for everyone.'

—NOURA ERAKAT,
Professor and author of *Justice for Some: Law and the Question of Palestine*

The Gaza Tribunal Panel
From left to right: Shahd Hammouri, Jeremy Corbyn
and Neve Gordon

The Gaza Tribunal

Britain's Complicity in Genocide

Jeremy Corbyn, Neve Gordon
and Shahd Hammouri

Afterword by Sally Rooney

PLUTO PRESS

First published 2026 by Pluto Press
New Wing, Somerset House, Strand, London WC2R 1LA
and Pluto Press, Inc.
1930 Village Center Circle, 3-834, Las Vegas, NV 89134

www.plutobooks.com

A CIP catalogue record for this book is available from the British Library

978-0-7453-5319-7 (paperback)
978-0-7453-5317-3 (.epub)
978-0-7453-5318-0 (.pdf)

Cover design by Melanie Patrick
Typeset by Jamie Bowman

Printed in the United Kingdom

EU GPSR Authorised Representative
LOGOS EUROPE, 9 rue Nicolas Poussin,
17000, LA ROCHELLE, France
Email: contact@logoseurope.eu

Contents

Preface

Jeremy Corbyn

Such an inquiry would be unnecessary as there is no confusion about UK military operations in Gaza ... There is no need for such an inquiry as proposed by this bill and therefore the government will oppose it.

In June 2025, I presented a Private Members' Bill to Parliament, calling for an independent, public inquiry into Britain's involvement in Israel's military operations in Gaza.[1] By that time, Israel had killed more than 55,000 Palestinians. Thousands more were missing under the rubble, buried by the moral and political cowardice of governments around the world – including our own. I wanted to know what equipment, arms and weapons had been supplied to Israel by the UK government. I wanted to know what RAF bases in Cyprus were being used for. I wanted to know what happened to all that intelligence that was picked up from the numerous RAF flights over Gaza. I wanted to know the UK's definition of genocide, and crucially what legal advice was sought and provided.

The Bill had the support of more than 50 MPs, alongside numerous human rights organisations. So, what did the government do? They blocked it. They even went to the trouble of writing me a letter, explaining that there was 'no need' for an inquiry. The government told me that an inquiry would be 'unnecessary' since 'there is no confusion about UK military operations in Gaza'. This staggering response followed months of evasion, obfuscation and outright refusal from government ministers to answer the many, many questions that MPs had been asking about the UK's involvement.

It's not complicated: if the government had nothing to hide, it wouldn't need to block our efforts to expose the truth. And if the government wasn't going to organise an open public inquiry, then it was left for us to do it ourselves. That is why we hosted the Gaza Tribunal: to expose the truth about Britain's complicity in war crimes, crimes against humanity and genocide.

Over the course of two days, Dr Shahd Hammouri, Professor Neve Gordon and I heard from a range of witnesses, whistle-blowers and experts. I am very grateful to Shahd and Neve for agreeing to host the Tribunal with me. Shahd's powerful opening speech, which she has adapted in Chapter 1, is a window into her extensive expertise in international law, her refreshingly decolonial approach, and the profoundly human voice that resonates through her courageous research. Neve Gordon brings a lifetime of insight into international human rights and humanitarian law to the Tribunal. As a consistently brave voice against Israeli colonial violence, he also brings a lifetime of solidarity. Together, Shahd and Neve are on the frontier of the legal liberation front – and their refusal to conform will continue to inspire countless others to build a kinder, more human world.

Thank you for your incredible work and the great friendship we have developed.

I also want to take this opportunity to thank the witnesses for their powerful testimonies, which will serve as a historical repository of evidence for generations to come. You have revealed the truth on so many things that have been hidden by much of the mainstream media and, indeed, by our government.

I want to say a particular thank you to the Palestinian speakers. They have witnessed the annihilation of their homes, their land and their people. They all have friends and family members who are suffering in Gaza, in the West Bank, in the Jordan Valley and in the refugee camps. And yet they still have the resilience to share the truth with the world. I think we should just hold our hands and our hearts out to all of the Palestinians that have made such an enormous contribution to this Tribunal.

We decided to host the Tribunal in Church House in Westminster. In 1945, this building hosted the first meeting of the United Nations Preparatory Commission to establish the security council. It also hosted the UN war crimes commission, which was collecting documents to be later used in Nuremberg.

Nine years ago, I used this building to present an apology to the military families of those that had lost loved ones in the war in Iraq. I issued that apology on behalf of the Labour Party for the failings of that government over taking this country to war in Iraq, detailed in Sir John Chilcot's report. The report found serious failings within the British government, who ignored the warnings of millions of ordinary people.

The Chilcot report did not come out of nowhere. It came after years and years of sustained pressure from MPs and campaigners to demand the truth. In the aftermath of the Iraq War, several attempts were made to establish an inquiry surrounding the conduct of British military operations. The government of the day spent many years resisting those attempts. Just like Iraq, the government is doing everything it can to protect itself from scrutiny. Just like Iraq, we do not need the government's permission to expose the truth.

We know this Tribunal will not be able to bring about justice by itself. That is why I will continue to push for a full, official, independent public inquiry into any and all cooperation between the UK and Israel since October 2023. And that is why I have written to the International Criminal Court, inviting them to look at the contents of this book and interview government ministers regarding their complicity in war crimes, crimes against humanity and genocide. Only then can we do what the inquiries into the Iraq War never did: bring about real accountability and real justice.

Over the past two years, a genocide has been live-streamed across the world. The equivalent of both of the post-war nuclear weapons have been dropped on 2 million people in Gaza. At the present time, there are more than a million tonnes of rubble for each inhabitant of Gaza. It will take years until we know the full scale of destruction. Even now, however, the level of suffering we have seen should haunt humanity forever. Entire families wiped out; limbs strewn across the street; mothers screaming for their children buried under the rubble; human beings torn to pieces; doctors performing amputations without anaesthetic; and children picking grass and dirt from the ground, thinking that they might find something edible.

Millions have reacted with horror as they have watched, in real time on television and on their phones, children being bombed and starved to death. In the words of Francesca

Albanese, UN Special Rapporteur on the situation of human rights in the Palestinian territories occupied since 1967, 'Palestine today is a crime scene.'

For many, the recent horrors in Gaza may have been the first time they have even heard of Palestine, let alone demonstrated for its freedom. It is tragically ironic that, for the millions of people who have been horrified by the images on their TV screens, Palestine has been put on the map only because Israel has attempted to wipe Palestine from it. Those who have been awakened by the genocide know this. Indeed, their exposure to Palestinian suffering has often been accompanied by the express realisation that they have been suffering for decades in relative silence. The genocide was not the beginning. It was a wake-up call: not only to the oppression of the Palestinian people but also to the urgency and permanency of the Palestinian cause.

Throughout its existence, Palestine has been sold short by every Western country and, if we're honest about it, every single neighbouring country. All the more remarkable, then, to witness the recent growth of the global movement for Palestine, and the enormous shift in public opinion over the past few years. With notable exceptions, this hasn't come from nation states. The real support for Palestinians comes from popular movements around the world. From London to Lagos, Johannesburg to Jakarta, and Stockholm to Sydney, the genocide in Gaza has kickstarted a global movement for Palestine. This global movement has stood up in the face of appalling levels of criminalisation and demonisation from governments and the media alike. The abuse heaped on pro-Palestinian protestors is reminiscent of the treatment of Vietnam War peace campaigners 50 years ago. Well, today, we know who was on the right side of history.

Palestinian solidarity is not a phase. It is not a temporary campaign. It is not fleeting. It is a lifelong struggle for justice, dignity and freedom. I have lost count of the number of demonstrations I have been on in solidarity with the Palestinian people. Each time, I go with the memories of Palestine at the forefront of my mind. And I endeavour to quote at least one Palestinian in any speech I give. In my mind, it's important to amplify the lived experiences of those enduring occupation, apartheid and genocide. That is what solidarity with the people of Palestine means.

This kind of solidarity comes in many shapes and sizes. Solidarity can look like Boycott, Divestment and Sanctions campaigns. It can look like national and global conferences. It can look like a protest. Above all, solidarity is a willingness to listen and learn from those whose daily life is one of oppression and violence. Our role – our duty – is to support the people of Palestine living under occupation. I don't know what the future holds any more than anybody else does, but I do know that it is up to the Palestinian people to determine it for themselves.

Over the course of my activities, I have witnessed the routine disregard for the humanity of Palestinians. Mass starvation cannot happen in a world where Palestinians are treated as equal human beings. Genocide cannot happen in a world where Palestinian lives matter. Apartheid cannot happen in a world where Palestinians have an inalienable right to self-determination. That's why I have always believed that it is for the Palestinian people – and only them – to decide their own future.

Palestinian solidarity did not begin with the genocide in Gaza. Likewise, it cannot end now. Not least because Israel continues to murder Palestinians behind the façade of a sham ceasefire. As Israel continues to murder, dispossess, coerce and deny Palestinians the means to live a dignified life in their homeland, it has never been more important to mobilise for Palestinian liberation.

We must continue to demand an end to all military cooperation with Israel. That includes all arms exports, surveillance technologies, surveillance flights, intelligence exchange, training, joint operations and security cooperation.

We must continue to demand economic sanctions, the suspension of trade agreements with Israel, and a ban on all settlement products and services until it ends its illegal occupation. All public contracts should be reviewed to prevent public institutions and funds from supporting Israel's illegal occupation. The government should issue widespread sanctions against senior members of the Israeli government and military.

We must continue to demand an end to the criminalisation of anti-genocide protest and the de-proscription of Palestine Action.

We must continue to support international efforts to enforce the ICJ ruling (July 2024) regarding Israel's illegal occupation of Palestinian territories, as well as South Africa's submission at the ICJ in the case against Israel (January 2024).

We must continue to demand more support for Palestinian-led initiatives to rebuild Gaza, particularly in the health, education and food production sectors. Funding to UNRWA must be restored as part of efforts to significantly expand humanitarian support for people in Gaza and demand that it be allowed to operate in the areas that Israel occupied in 1967.

And we must continue to urge all states, including the UK, to take all possible measures and enforce policies to end Israeli occupation of the State of Palestine and remove obstacles to the realisation of the right of the Palestinian people to self-determination.

Over my lifetime, it's been my privilege to go to Palestine on nine different occasions. I've been in all parts of Palestine. I've had some wonderful meetings with some wonderful people. I've heard some horror stories, but I've always been impressed by the fortitude, the culture, the determination and the civilisation of the Palestinian people, their poetry, their music, their art and everything else. And I've never forgotten going to primary schools in Jabalia refugee camp, talking to the children there, them reading the poetry they had written.

That school is destroyed. Many of those children will now be dead. And the hopes that they had for a life of peace, for a life where they could fulfil their ambitions, have sadly gone for those that have not survived. When I hear news of bombings in Gaza, I think about the schools I have visited and the people I met. I don't know if the children I met are still alive. I don't know. Every person in Gaza has a name and a face; we grieve for babies in incubators just as deeply as we grieve for middle-aged men killed crossing the road. In any case, we are mourning the theft of beautiful, creative lives. Artists whose paintings we will never see. Singers whose songs we will never sing. Authors whose books we will never read. Teachers whose lessons we will never learn. I am determined that in everything we do in solidarity with the Palestinian people, we emphasise their cultural strength, their poetry, their art, their music and above all their indomitable optimism.

In our discussions of Gaza, we always emphasise the horror stories. For as long as I can remember, Gaza has been reduced on our TV screens to a site of debris and despair. But underneath the rubble are the quiet, unremarkable foundations of our shared humanity. Morning coffee rounds, hot showers, shopping trips, card games and bedtime stories. Friendship, heartbreak, love, disappointment, boredom and suspense. Schools, mosques, theatres, universities, libraries, playgrounds and hospitals. Dreams, fears, cares and joys.

Each time I have visited Palestine, I am in awe of the resilience of a people under siege. We are presented with a view of the Palestinian people as being in a hopeless position. They're not. Their determination, their cultural strength, their community spirit and their belief in the cause of Palestine outweighs all of that. In my own constituency, the Palestinian owners of Archway's Café Metro, Faten and Mahmoud, often open their café to people in the evening to treat them to a Palestinian dinner, so that people can experience the country's culture through its food. Faten has lost many of her relatives in the genocide. All of her families' homes have been destroyed. 'Now I live in London,' Faten says, 'but my heart and soul remain with my family there. I wanted to do something from here. I organise these dinners to share our story in a different way – through food. Every bite carries a message that we, as Palestinians, have a history, a culture and an identity, and we are still holding on to life despite the devastation.'

When I think about my trips to Gaza, yes I remember the destruction. But I also remember the shoots of hope. Every available piece of ground was planted with fruit and vegetables. Small-scale markets were aplenty. Schools were full of children desperate to learn. The life of Palestinian people is unbelievably harsh and brutal, but we should find inspiration in their enduring strength, resilience and joy.

The Gaza Tribunal will help cement the government's legacy as an active participant in one of the greatest crimes of our time. I hope it will serve as a historical repository of evidence for generations to come. I hope it will help mobilise support for Palestinian liberation. And I hope it becomes a global model for campaigners everywhere attempting to hold their governments to account. The UK is not the only country to have facilitated genocide in Gaza. Israel relied on military, economic and political support from governments across the world – and all those who have played a role in this crime against humanity must be brought to justice.

We must not just be bystanders and witnesses of what has gone on. We have to be able to do something about it. That's why people march. That's why people meet. That's why people demonstrate. That's why people take legal action. And that's why we have tried to expose the truth, to bring to bear expert knowledge, to bring to bear principles of how we can help to alleviate the appalling suffering of the Palestinian people. Palestine is the cause of this generation. History will judge, very harshly, the role of the political and media class for their complicity in the attempted elimination of Palestine.

Many ask me why I keep demonstrating in the face of an establishment that – more often than not – refuses to listen. For me, we only need one reason: Palestinians are human beings who deserve to live in dignity. Surely that is enough to keep campaigning for their liberation – and for a world where all human beings, no matter their faith, can exist side-by-side in peace.

The genocide never ended. Neither, then, can our solidarity with a people yearning to survive. We will keep going until justice prevails in Gaza. It is the home of the Palestinian people – and long may it be so.

Introduction

On the 13 July 2024, Israel bombed the al-Mawasi camp in southern Gaza. A designated 'safe zone', al-Mawasi was home to 80,000 people who were trying to flee from bombardment. The airstrikes killed more than 90 Palestinians. It would take Britain's Labour government another six weeks to impose any arms restrictions on Israel at all. By that time, at least 41,000 Palestinians had been killed in Gaza, including 11,000 children. More than 96,000 people had been injured. Two-thirds of the buildings in Gaza had been destroyed. Eight months before the government's announcement, the International Court of Justice (ICJ) ruled that a plausible genocide was taking place and set into motion the obligation of all parties – including the UK – to prevent it.

When the government announced a partial suspension of arms export licences to Israel in September 2024, this was not the end of British complicity. It was the beginning of a new campaign of lies, evasion and obfuscation. Suspending around 30 arms export licences out of a total of 350, the government made one, huge, glaring omission: the continued supply of parts for Israel's F-35 jets. This included components that went to the United States to be sent on to Israel, and spare parts that went into the global stockpiles that may then go to Israel.

Approximately 15 per cent of every F-35 aircraft that is produced is made in the UK. The rear fuselage is made in Lancaster; the active interceptor system in Kent; durability testing in East Yorkshire; the ejector seats in Buckinghamshire; the weapons release mechanisms in Brighton. On the very same day that the Foreign Secretary announced the partial suspension, a report found that an F-35 was used to drop three 2,000-pound bombs in the al-Mawasi massacre.

The Gaza Tribunal reveals the truth about British complicity in genocide. This book is based on a two-day Tribunal, which took place in September 2025. Held in Church House, Westminster, 'The Gaza Tribunal' provided a platform for survivors, witnesses and whistle-blowers to uncover the devastating scope of Israel's crimes against humanity and the truth of Britain's involvement.

The Tribunal was hosted by the three of us: Jeremy Corbyn MP, Dr Shahd Hammouri and Professor Neve Gordon. Our responsibilities were to oversee the collection of evidence relating to Britain's complicity in genocide. Splitting the Tribunal up into four sections, we selected and invited witnesses to respond to one of the following questions: What has happened in Gaza?; What are Britain's legal responsibilities?; What has Britain done?; and Has Britain fulfilled its obligations? Listening to each witness in turn, we asked them follow-up questions about the information they had provided. The witness testimonies formed the basis of our conclusions, which we summarised in a report, published in early 2026. This book is based on that report – with expanded testimonies, updated conclusions and fresh recommendations.

This book is not an exhaustive investigation into Israel's crimes, not least because these crimes continued long after the

Tribunal concluded. Indeed, the day after the Tribunal ended, at least 68 Palestinians were killed and 362 others were injured in Israeli attacks. Since the announcement of the so-called ceasefire on 10 October 2025, through to late February 2026, Israel has killed more than 750 Palestinians and injured over 2,000.[2] Israeli authorities, along with American and British allies, have imposed on Palestinians a foreign governance system that ignores principles like sovereignty, self-determination and accountability.[3] In April 2025, the Israeli Knesset passed a new law effectively imposing the death penalty solely against Palestinians. UN experts described this as a 'discriminatory regime of capital punishment' which 'manifestly violated Israel's obligations under international human rights law'.

The Gaza Tribunal is predominantly concerned with events taking place from October 2023 to September 2025. We uncover evidence of British complicity across both the Conservative government (in office up until July 2024) and the Labour government (July 2024–to date). The Tribunal heard from international legal experts and UN officials, who outlined a range of legal obligations compelling Britain to prevent genocide and bring to an end Israel's illegal occupation of Palestine. The Tribunal heard from Palestinians, journalists and healthcare workers who have survived the genocide, and who spoke for themselves about the genocide that has been streamed live to our computers and phones. The Tribunal heard from whistle-blowers who described how the British government has created a culture of deceit to hide the truth. The Tribunal heard from a range of witnesses who proved beyond doubt: Britain has not just been complicit in genocide, it has been an active participant.

The Gaza Tribunal has been written collectively by Jeremy Shahd and Neve, unless specified. Before presenting the evidence from the Tribunal, each of the Tribunal's co-panellists outline the motivation for the Tribunal. Following on from the preface from Jeremy Corbyn, Chapter 1, by Shahd Hammouri, places the Gaza genocide in the context of Britain's 'low-intensity democracy' and decades-long practice of colonial erasure. In Chapter 2, Neve Gordon reflects on how his own Jewish faith and political education have shaped his opposition to genocide.

Chapters 3–6 document the devastating testimonies that were given at the Tribunal. In Chapter 3, witnesses describe in horrifying detail the human reality of displacement, ethnic cleansing and genocide. This includes, but is not limited to, the deliberate and near-total destruction of the healthcare system, the destruction of the education system, the targeting of journalists and the production of famine.

Chapter 4 details Britain's legal obligations, including the duty to prevent and punish genocide, and the duty to bring about an end to an illegal occupation. This chapter makes particular reference to a series of landmark rulings issued by the ICJ.

Chapter 5 reveals the scale of Britain's involvement in Israel's military operations in Gaza. This includes the sale, supply and transfer of weapons; the performance of Royal Air Force (RAF) surveillance flights over Gaza; the use of British air bases in facilitating the transport, refuelling and maintenance of military equipment; the provision of political and diplomatic support; the failure to impose sanctions on Israel or to use other economic and diplomatic instruments in adherence with its legal duty to bring about an end to Israel's illegal occupation.

Chapter 6 makes the following judgement: the British government has been complicit in war crimes, crimes against humanity and genocide committed by Israel. Based on the evidence provided, it is reasonable to conclude that the British government may even have been an active participant in these crimes.

The Conclusion describes how the 'Gaza Doctrine' has metastasised to other areas in West Asia. This is a symptom of tectonic shifts in the global world order reflecting the decay of hegemonic powers, which exert maximum force in a desperate attempt to salvage their dominance. We further maintain that the complicity of the British government and some of its European allies in the genocide in Gaza have both enabled the doctrine and set the stage for the complete erosion of the post-Second World War international legal order, as well as the norms obliging warring parties to protect civilians and civilian sites. A 'might makes right' system has unfolded before our very eyes – and the British government is partly to blame. In a devastating and damning afterword, Sally Rooney asks the question: Having betrayed their own people and made a mockery of international law, what exactly do countries like the UK have to show for it?

This book cannot simply exist for its own sake. The UK government should be investigated for its complicity in genocide – and it should cooperate with all domestic and international mechanisms of accountability. Let us be very clear: when we say that the 'British government' is complicit, that means government ministers and officials who have authorised the continuation of military, economic and political support. Today, schoolchildren are taught about history's worst crimes against humanity. They are asked to reflect on how these crimes possibly could have occurred. And they learn the names of political figures that endorsed or enabled such atrocities. In the near future, our history books will shame those in our government who could have stopped the genocide in Gaza but facilitated it instead.

1

In Defiance of Illusions

An edited transcript of Dr Shahd Hammouri's speeches at The Gaza Tribunal

What has happened in Gaza is not surprising; it was a foreseeable bloodbath. Each time I try to grasp what genocide truly means, or perhaps what it feels like, I experience a sense of dissociation: this cannot be real, my mind insists. This level of pain and suffering, repeated over more than three years, with the entire world watching, feels impossible to comprehend. Atrocity is not new in human history; what is new is the scale of the spectacle, the normalisation of carnage deemed acceptable by the dominant global order, with the UK at its centre. This prolonged condition has poisoned the global consciousness, shifting the boundaries of what counts as 'acceptable carnage' further toward the extreme end of sadistic violence.

The problem is not simply what the UK government has or has not done since 2023; it is, perhaps, the illusion that it can claim any moral superiority at all. This illusion is central to the exercise of power on a global scale within the prevailing post-Second World War order. After the Second World War, the victors set the rules of the game. While documents such as the UN Charter sought to establish higher standards for international relations, this framework, anchored in the language of peace and security, was ultimately constrained by the interests of those same victors. For example, although it advanced certain human rights norms, it also constructed a global economic system grounded in coercion through sustained dependency.

Efforts to challenge this status quo were met with coercion, whether physical, economic or diplomatic. For example, states that sought to develop their economies through nationalisation, in the name of sovereignty over natural resources, were often subjected to attack or economic sanctions. This order entrenched inequality while rewarding elites across the globe. Such inequality may not appear as immediately gruesome as genocide, but it does not require much imagination to see the forms of systemic violence it produces for the global majority.

The status quo is predicated on colonial erasure. To claim moral superiority, one must erase one's bloodied past and present, and the lessons of history from the standpoint of the oppressed must be buried. Whenever I confront lawyers or state officials in the Global North with questions surrounding mass atrocity, I find myself repeatedly reminding some of them that this is not an exceptional historical occurrence confined to the past. For them, atrocities only happened in the past, predominantly exemplified by the Holocaust. What this narrative hides is that the Holocaust was colonial violence inverted inward into Europe, or, as Césaire calls it, the boomerang effect of colonisation.[4] The same mechanisms of violence were perfected over the years on the bodies of Kenyans, Libyans, Indigenous Americans and Australians, Haitians and many others before being applied against marginalised populations on mainland Europe. When it comes to the present, the suffering of the Global Majority under the whip of the neocolonial formation of subordination is equally erased as an irrelevant consideration. Because, according to the logic of the current world order, their death and suffering are acceptable waste in the equation of the accumulation of power and capital.[5] Without reckoning with that history and this present, the foreseeability of the genocide in Gaza was, of course, invisible to many.

Liberal international lawyers often celebrate the post-Second World War order as an era of peace, urging critics to accept its flaws as the price of stability. Yet this position rests on a profound illusion. Many of the wars since the Second World War have been waged against those whose lives are treated as less worthy, the colonised, resisting domination or fighting wars shaped by colonial and imperial interests across Algeria, Libya, Korea, Vietnam, Liberia, Haiti, Syria and beyond. A closer examination of wars during this period reveals recurring patterns of foreign intervention and the decisive role of capital in structuring the conditions for mass violence.

At the local level, the architects of the post-Second World War order claimed moral superiority through the language of the rule of law. From the Global South, one watches on television the clean streets, orderly institutions and functioning services, and is told that the reason these conditions do not exist at home is that one's government and people do not respect the so-called Western values of democracy and human rights. In other words, Latin Americans, Africans and Asians are said to be 'behind' simply because they lack the same values. What this narrative obscures is the relationship between accumulation, on one side, and dispossession, on the other, produced through complex histories and structural inequalities.

The genocide has challenged this illusion and revealed to the masses the confines of claims to democracy and human rights. We were told that democracy is a central value of the British system of governance, yet the most basic tenets of democratic rule were nowhere to be seen during the genocide. Democracy requires a commitment to honesty, the rule of law and effective participation in decision-making. England, as Samir Amin notes, is governed by what he calls 'low-intensity democracy'.[6] Public debate and representative politics are limited to the boundaries accepted by the establishment, namely, the economic and military elites of this country invested in maintaining the global status quo and its rules of the game.

Recognising the danger of this situation, state officials and prominent media outlets actively and knowingly distorted public perception of reality in Gaza. They endorsed atrocity propaganda, used narratives that dehumanised and diminished Palestinian, Lebanese and Iranian lives, and at times bluntly denied lived reality. They did the same with South Africa, India, Afghanistan, Ireland and Iraq – the list goes on. They do the same when talking about tax havens, corporate regulation and the environment. They misrepresented their historical, economic, military and political role in the genocide and the systems of domination that made the bloodbath inevitable. They fragmented the picture. At times, they even had the audacity to claim that they are doing this in the name of 'saving the oppressed'. They threw a blanket of dehumanisation over the whole population by uttering the magic words – 'Hamas', 'Hezbollah', 'Iran'. And they asked the British public not to contemplate the chain of causality, or dare to look behind the blanket to see the humanity of a subjugated population.

The government did this in the name of the British public, claiming that this was the only viable foreign policy. I would like to believe that if people were truly presented with the truth of what is happening on the ground today: if they could conceptualise, imagine, perceive and feel the sound of a child screaming as his leg is amputated without anaesthetic; the heat of a British-made drone exploding in a tent; the smell of burnt human flesh; the over three years of endless horror lived by millions of people in the region after a long project of settler colonisation, I would like to believe that none of them would want any role in causing it at any cost.

Meanwhile, in the courts of this country and the offices of governmental legal advisers, geopolitical alliances were favoured over the basic tenets of national and international law. In the streets, persistent demonstrations by hundreds of thousands, if not millions, of British people asking for the most basic demands were systematically denied, undermined and demonised. These systems are legitimised in the name of serving the British public. Yet they failed to protect a basic right: the right not to be complicit in a genocide. A right that many rightly invoked, a right that might seem intangible in a world system that marginalises meaning and human connection. The reality is, to be a human in the UK during the genocide meant risking your freedom, your job, your source of income in the name of clearing your consciousness from the realisation that you are on the privileged end of a structure of dispossession that has crossed the margin of systemic violence to open-ended carnage.

We were denied our right to save ourselves, our humanity, our collective consciousness and our search for meaning, less than basic.

Our witnesses affirmed that the British government does indeed have the knowledge and capacity to understand the reality on the ground. They also affirmed that the British government is undertaking surveillance flights that support the ongoing genocide. They told us that the government has access to information generated through the most advanced forms of intelligence, and yet it continues to deny what it knows and refuses to share that information with the public. Tactics of delay, intimidation, contradiction and politicisation of legal proceedings have left civil servants under pressure, condemned if they speak and condemned if they do not.

These are the questions I ask my students: what is the position of a civil servant who can see, knowingly, the complicity of their own government before them, yet risks losing their livelihood if they dare to say a word? The British government has not only denied the British people's right not to be complicit in a genocide, but it has also denied its civil servants the capacity to engage with and apply the law.

This is a masterpiece of war crimes, a masterpiece of joint criminal enterprise.

The representatives of the British state, as well as corporations, seem to have forgotten basic history: the truth of atrocity will come. Perhaps they hope it will come too late, or that it will never come at all. Our task here today is to ensure that truth arrives in the present. I say this with utter confidence because I know that reckoning with the reality of what is happening in West Asia, and the post-Second World War order more generally, is imminent. That reality has scarred the consciousness of humanity and caused untold sorrow. But what if it will come only after it is too late? As Omar El Akkad says: 'One day, when it's safe, when there's no personal downside to calling a thing what it is, when it's too late to hold anyone accountable, everyone will have always been against this.'[7] This document seeks to resist this. We hope that this Tribunal brings us one step closer to the inevitable reckoning for the most atrocious things we have witnessed in our lifetimes.

We place this document in your hands today as an act of resistance. If the whole world order denied Gaza a loaf of bread, then the only path to justice starts with challenging the whole world order. This document studies the extreme case of how the illusion of moral superiority is sustained during a live-broadcast genocide. Or in other words, how a government can be complicit in a genocide, and deny it with a straight face. It seeks to document history, vindicate reality and offer lessons learned in blood and gore to future generations. Our mission is to bring an inevitable reckoning with the truth a step closer. This document is anchored in hope that we can aspire to a global world order based on structural equality and the negation of coercive politics. A global world order that sheds away illusions, and builds on justice as seen from the standpoint of those most precarious. These aspirational dreams are our duty to Gaza – the dream has to be proportional to the pain endured. The soil of Gaza, drenched in the blood of martyrs, is fertile ground for the blooming of global movements anchored in clear-sighted vision of justice that sheds away all illusions.

2

Justice, Justice You Shall Pursue

An edited transcript of Professor Neve Gordon's speeches at The Gaza Tribunal

We have gathered here today to interrogate Israel's violations of international humanitarian law and the Genocide Convention in both the Gaza Strip and the West Bank, and to investigate the UK government's complicity in these violations.

My motivation for being here has to do with my upbringing. I was born and raised in Israel. Every Saturday until the age of 18, my father, my older brother and I would attend the local Orthodox synagogue in the southern city of Israel, Beer-Sheva. As you can imagine, it was not always the way I wanted to spend my Saturday mornings, but I did learn two important lessons from that experience – lessons that I still carry with me.

First, I learned that the Jewish prophets looked upon reality with eyes wide open and were never afraid to speak truth to power. Frequently, their harshest criticism was directed against their own people, the Israelites. The prophets were often ignored, ridiculed or aggressively scorned. But they never bowed down and persisted to speak the truth. Second, I learned from the book *Devarim* (Deuteronomy in English) that we are called upon to pursue justice. 'Justice, justice you shall pursue.' The repetition of the word justice underscores both the obligation to pursue justice relentlessly and vigorously, and that the pursuit for justice must be carried out through just means. Thus, as I see it, one key role of this Tribunal is to follow these two principles or, if you will, commandments: namely, to look at reality head on and to speak truth, and to do both in the pursuit of justice.

In my 20s, I went on to university to study political theory, and one of the thinkers I read was the Jewish political philosopher, Hannah Arendt. In addition to my early upbringing, the time I spent studying Arendt taught me a number of lessons that I also still carry with me. Again, two lessons seem to be particularly relevant for this hearing.

The first has to do with responsibility and judgement. Arendt emphasises the importance of individual responsibility and accentuates its role in restoring human dignity in resisting injustice, and in realising freedom. She also states that the act of judgement is fundamental to personal responsibility. It is, she maintains, our responsibility to judge political actions. Our judgement, however, must not be limited to the actions of the immediate perpetrators but also be extended to the wider system of complicity that enables the perpetrators to carry out crimes. Indeed, when reporting on the trial of Adolf Eichmann in Jerusalem, she argued that responsibility is more complex than simply blaming the individual who pulls the trigger or the person who signs the extermination order. The entire system of political conformity that aids and abets monstrous acts is also culpable.

The second important lesson Arendt taught me has to do with the possibility of punishment. Human action, she reminds us, is often unpredictable and can disrupt and violently destroy life. Both forgiveness and punishment can, however, act as correctives to this inherent unpredictability and frailty. While forgiveness is vital for human interaction within our common world, Arendt famously wrote that humans are unable to forgive what they cannot punish. The possibility of punishment in her view is necessary because without it we cannot distinguish between permissible and impermissible acts. In other words, without the possibility of punishment, we cannot assert that genocide is impermissible. When we cannot categorise acts as punishable, then, according to Arendt, everything is allowed, which would mean that we cannot judge actions and we cannot restore the stability of our common world after a horrific wrong has been committed.

These two lessons should, in my opinion, also inform the Tribunal. First, the idea that when judging we must transcend the actions of the immediate perpetrators and consider the wider system of complicity that enables the crimes. Second, that the possibility of punishment is necessary both for restoring human dignity and for the possibility of any future forgiveness. It is, I believe, our responsibility to the Palestinians in Gaza, the West Bank and East Jerusalem who have been subjected to monstrous violence as well as to their brethren in the diaspora to heed these two lessons from Hannah Arendt, while also adopting the lessons of the prophets: speaking truth to power and pursuing justice. I firmly believe that this Tribunal will lead us towards that goal.

This Tribunal began with wrenching testimonies.

We heard about the mass assassination of civilians alongside the systematic attacks on the Palestinian healthcare system, the system responsible for saving and sustaining life in the Gaza Strip. We heard about cancer patients and dialysis patients dying because they cannot access treatments. We heard testimonies of doctors who treated children whose bodies were burnt, whose limbs were detached and whose faces were scorched. We learned how doctors were forced to carry out surgeries without the necessary medical equipment, how patients have undergone surgeries without painkillers, and how the screams of men, women and children continue to haunt healthcare staff for days and months after they leave the Gaza Strip. We heard how healthcare workers have been assassinated at a much higher rate than civilians, and how their families have also been targeted.

We heard how Israel banned all foreign news journalists from entering Gaza, and within days of the onslaught the Israeli military eliminated the media institutions in the Strip, damaging or destroying news agencies, radio stations and transmission towers, while razing internet cables across the territory. We heard how the military also created target banks and circulated assassination lists of Palestinian journalists, killing those whose job it is to report the facts on the ground, to bear witness and to provide evidence of war crimes, crimes against humanity and genocide. We heard that more journalists were killed in Gaza than the number of journalists who died in the US Civil War, the First and Second World Wars, the Korean War, the Vietnam War, the wars in Yugoslavia in the 1990s and 2000s, and the post-9/11 war in Afghanistan combined.

We heard about famine and about how Israel is depriving Palestinians of objects indispensable for their survival. We heard about how mothers and fathers search for food for their hungry children, and how often these children go to sleep hungry. We heard of babies dying because Israel prohibits the entry of formula. We heard about the pattern of wounds and injuries sustained by hungry boys and girls lining up for food at the gates of the famine profiteering organisation, the Gaza Humanitarian Foundation. We heard of children dreaming of having a clean cup of water.

We heard how boys and men aged 15–70 are considered killable, regardless of who they are. We heard of mass graves, of snipers shooting at people as if they were prey.

We heard how the Israeli military has categorised 86 per cent of the Gaza Strip as a military zone, pushing the civilian population into what it considers to be humanitarian zones. We heard how Palestinians have been killed on the way to these zones and often within them. We heard that 90 per cent of Gaza's population has been displaced, most of the population many times over, and some even more than ten times. We heard that there is no safe space in Gaza.

We heard how Israel has destroyed almost all of the schools in Gaza and every single university. We heard how children are denied access to education. We heard about the biosphere of genocide that Israel is creating, and how when buildings are bombed or bulldozed, their debris –wiring, solvents, insulation, asbestos – release toxic chemicals into the soil and release lead and arsenic deep underground. We heard of 'ungrounding Gaza' and that the harm Israel has been generating is magnitudes greater than what is currently known, and how it will affect the population for decades and generations to come.

We also heard from lawyers and genocide experts. We heard how Israel has violated the most fundamental principles and clauses of international humanitarian law, the principles of distinction and proportionality, and that the pattern of its conducts comprise crimes against humanity. We heard from lawyers that the occupation itself is illegal and not only the conduct within it, and from genocide experts that what Israel has been carrying out in Gaza meets the threshold of the Genocide Convention and how there is no doubt about this in the international scholarly community. We heard that only partisan supporters of Israel think otherwise today.

We heard that one of the lessons of the Holocaust is that if we want to understand genocide, we need to listen to those who experienced it on the ground and not to powerful states. No one would dream of asking the Nazi's how they treated the Jews. It is the testimonies of Jews who suffered in the concentration camps that helps us understand what happened in the camps.

We also heard that genocide is always carried out through genocide denial.

We heard about the UK government's line of defence, about the claim made by UK politicians that Israel's intentions are not clear and therefore it is not obvious that its military has violated international law. Witnesses have highlighted Israel's intentions – which are not secret; indeed, these witnesses have emphasised that intentions can be deduced not only from statements made by political and military leaders but also from the systematic patterns of attacks. These witnesses showed, in other words, that the UK government's claim about intentions is nothing more than a ploy and that there is no doubt that every single day for almost two years Israel has been committing egregious violations of international law.

We have heard, however, that even members of the Labour Party have not received access to the reports made by the UK legal departments.

We also heard how, despite its legal obligations, the UK government has not acted with due diligence and has not stopped the transfer of F-35 parts manufactured in the UK to Israel, and how it has been supporting Israeli military operations through reconnaissance flights from military bases in Cyprus. We heard how the UK has been supporting Israel in an array of diplomatic fora, and about the significance of this support for the continuance of the genocide. The fact that the UK government has kept open lines of communication with Israel but is unwilling to talk to Palestinians speaks volumes.

We heard that British citizens who are living in the West Bank or serving in the military in Gaza are in violation of international law and legally speaking should be arrested when re-entering the UK.

Ultimately, we heard about how a culture of deception has taken over the UK government in every aspect of its handling of Israel and the genocide it is perpetrating in Gaza. We have heard that this culture of deception is produced through the circulation of misleading information, half-truths, disingenuous responses and outright lies that are designed to cover up crimes. We have learned that this deception is bolstered through the cooperation of the Israeli and UK intelligence communities, through pressures of corporations that profit from war-making, through different lobbying groups, and through politicians who are working at their behest.

We will now have to examine all the evidence put before us. And while the efforts to cover up UK complicity and involvement in genocide will no doubt continue, I am confident that truth will be exposed and Justice will ultimately prevail.

3

Genocide

We have all seen the images: mass graves; mutilated bodies; families in tents being burned alive; people getting shot as they queue for a bag of flour.

At the time of writing, the official death toll in Gaza had exceeded 73,000, of whom at least 21,000 are children.[8] These conservative figures do not include an untold number of people lost under the rubble, or those whose deaths have not been recorded or reported to the Palestinian health authorities. At least 200,000 more have been injured; Gaza is now the home of the largest cohort of child amputees in the world. More than 80 per cent of the buildings in Gaza have been either damaged or destroyed, including more than 90 per cent of housing, 97 per cent of schools, 33 of 36 hospitals, and all the universities.[9] More than 95 per cent of Gaza's agricultural land has been rendered unusable.[10] At least 1.9 million people across the Gaza Strip have been displaced.[11] Right now, over a million Palestinians are living in squalid tents without electricity, running water or a sewage system.

This chapter documents the reality of genocide through the eyes and ears of Palestinians, medics, journalists, campaigners and legal experts who testified at the Gaza Tribunal. First, however, it is crucial to explain how this genocidal reality began long before October 2023.

Balfour

The UK's complicity and genocide did not start on October 7th. It did not start on the 15th of May 1948. It started on the day [British administrators] stepped foot into Palestine.

—HALA SABBAH

British involvement in Palestine can be traced back to the 1917 Balfour Declaration and the 1922 British Mandate. Even though in 1918 there were about 750,000 Palestinians of various religions and 56,000 predominantly Jewish immigrants who had moved to Palestine under the auspices of the Zionist project, the British government promised to establish a homeland for the Jews within the territory it had occupied, mentioning the hundreds of thousands of indigenous Palestinians in both the Declaration and Mandate only in passing, referring to them as 'non-Jews'.[12]

During the 1936–1939 Palestinian revolt against British rule, the colonial military brutally suppressed the uprising.[13] From 1947 to 1949, when 750,000 Palestinians out of a total population of 900,000 either fled or were expelled by Zionist forces from their villages, towns and cities in a massive act of dispossession and expropriation known as al-Nakba (meaning catastrophe), the British government failed to prevent ethnic cleansing or to ensure that the refugees be allowed to return to their homes after the war had subsided.[14] The British government even refrained from criticising the fledgling Israeli state when it destroyed 500 Palestinian villages and built 350 Jewish-only settlements on, or in proximity to, these villages' remains.[15]

In this context, the United Nations General Assembly adopted a partition plan for Palestine in Resolution 181 (II) (1947), effectively paving the way for the colonial expropriation of Palestinian land and mass dispossession. This was followed by the recognition of the state of Israel in May 1949, with no recognition of a Palestinian state.

Today, three-quarters of Gaza's population of 2.3 million consists of refugees and descendants of refugees who fled from Jaffa, Asqalan and scores of towns and villages in 1948.[16]

Since then, Israel has continuously and systematically adopted colonial policies and practices that seek to erase, dispossess and expropriate the Palestinians. Meanwhile, successive British governments have remained silent, providing support to Israeli governments that systematically abuse Palestinians' rights. Following the 1967 occupation of the West Bank, Gaza Strip and East Jerusalem, and the further displacement of hundreds of thousands of Palestinians, Israel established 21 illegal Jewish settlements in the Gaza Strip and used these settlements to control most of the seashore as well as to create a wedge between the northern and southern parts of this narrow sliver of land.[17]

By 1987, Israel had managed to restrict Palestinians to 60 per cent of the land in Gaza and began a process of caging Palestine's population within Gaza. In 1989, it introduced a policy of only allowing people with magnetic cards – which contained coded information about each person's 'security background', taxes and utility bills – to exit the region.

In 1991, within the context of the US–British–Iraq War, it implemented the first 'hermetic closure', which sealed off the Gaza Strip for long periods. In the midst of the Oslo process (a series of peace negotiations between Israel and the Palestine Liberation Organization (PLO) starting in 1993), Israel built a patrol road and a series of fences – totalling 54 kilometres – to close off the border between the Gaza Strip and Israel, leaving only four passages connecting the two regions (two of which operate in one direction only, from Israel to Gaza) and one more connecting Gaza with Egypt.

In 2004, Israeli Prime Minister Ariel Sharon decided that it was no longer feasible to deploy hundreds of Israeli soldiers to secure the 8,000 Jewish settlers in the Gaza Strip and decided to withdraw Israeli troops. Sharon thought that by implementing a unilateral 'disengagement plan', Israel could present itself as having de-occupied Gaza. This, in turn, would help separate Gaza from the West Bank and allow Israel to fortify its West Bank settlements and entrench its control of the land.

In 2005, the Israeli government dismantled the Jewish settlements in Gaza and redeployed its troops to the border. Israel subsequently transformed and intensified its control of the enclave from a distance, building military bases just outside the Gaza Strip, setting up remotely controlled machine guns on watchtowers, increasing the use of drones, and establishing a buffer zone 150 to 500 metres wide that eats up agricultural land while mandating farmers to limit themselves to short leafy crops such as spinach, radish and lettuce, presumably to avoid blocking soldiers' views.[18]

Two years after the 2005 withdrawal, Hamas was elected as the governing party in the Gaza Strip. In response, Israel implemented a permanent military blockade on Gaza, cordoning off the population in what many commentators have described as an 'open-air prison'. Recently, the International Court of Justice (ICJ), the highest court in the land, issued a ruling that the occupation of Palestinian territories, including the Gaza Strip, and not merely Israeli conduct within it is illegal and must end immediately.[19]

On 7 October 2023, after 17 years of Israeli siege and multiple rounds of deadly attacks on Gaza where countless atrocities were committed against the besieged population, the Al Qassam Brigades and other Palestinian armed groups infiltrated Israeli military bases, kibbutzim, towns and the Nova music festival. On that day, 1,139 people, including 375 Israeli security personnel and 764 civilians, of whom up to 38 were children, were massacred, while 251 soldiers and civilians were taken as captives and hostages. According to the UN's Independent International Commission of Inquiry, strong evidence indicates that Israel bears partial responsibility for some of these killings by invoking the 'Hannibal Directive'. This controversial military protocol prioritises neutralising captors, even if it entails killing the civilians being held hostage.[20] Israeli leaders immediately made it clear that they intended to respond with eliminatory forms of violence against Gaza's population.

On 9 October, following two days of extensive aerial bombing by Israel, the country's minister of energy and infrastructure, Israel Katz, announced that he had ordered water, electricity and fuel to be cut off. 'What was,' he said, 'will not be.' The same day, the Defence Minister, Yoav Gallant, demanded a 'complete siege' of the enclave, stating that: 'there will be no food, there will be no fuel'. His reasoning has since become notorious: 'we are fighting human animals', which suggests that he thought that the Geneva Conventions are not applicable in a war against Palestinians.[21] On 17 October, the National Security Minister, Itamar Ben-Gvir, insisted that 'as long as Hamas does not release the hostages in its hands... not an ounce of humanitarian aid' would enter Gaza – only 'hundreds of tons of explosives from the Air Force'.[22] The next day, Prime Minister Benjamin Netanyahu put the matter in similarly stark terms: 'We will not allow humanitarian assistance in the form of food and medicines from our territory to the Gaza Strip.'[23]

In response to the clearly articulated intention of grave violations of international law, Britain maintained a position of 'unequivocally backing Israel's right to defend itself'.[24] Notably, Keir Starmer, the Labour Party leader at the time, publicly stated that Israel has the right to cut off water and electricity to the besieged population of Gaza.[25]

These were all declarations of an intent to deprive the Palestinians in Gaza 'of objects indispensable to their survival, including wilfully impeding relief supplies' – the legal definition of 'using starvation of civilians as a method of warfare', a crime against international law under the Rome Statute and a clear warning sign of a potential genocide.[26] Israeli newspapers, television and social media, meanwhile, were saturated with calls to destroy the population, in whole or in part: to 'erase' Gaza, 'flatten' it, turn it 'into Dresden'.[27]

On 13 October 2023 – the day that Israeli authorities ordered 1.1 million people in northern Gaza to evacuate their homes within 24 hours – the country's president, Isaac Herzog, said publicly: 'It is an entire nation out there that is responsible... It is not true this rhetoric about civilians not aware, not involved.'[28] For Herzog, there were no innocent civilians in

Gaza. Echoing this sentiment, Netanyahu promised that the Israeli military would strike 'forcefully everywhere', in a war that he described as 'a struggle between the children of light and the children of darkness, between humanity and the law of the jungle'.[29]

In effect, Israeli leaders notified the public of their intention to disregard the basic distinction between civilians and combatants, choosing to attack the Palestinian people as a people. In the meantime, the British media predominantly retained an overwhelmingly good-faith reading of Israeli sources and endorsed narratives that eased the justification of mass atrocities against the Palestinians.

After two years of Israel's genocidal campaign, Israeli forces had completely or partially destroyed 89 per cent of the buildings in Rafah, 84 per cent of the buildings in the northern Gaza Strip and 78 per cent of the buildings in Gaza City.[30] The human cost is difficult to quantify. In January 2026, a senior Israeli military official accepted the estimate of the Gaza Health Ministry that at least 71,000 Palestinians have been killed, of whom at least 20,000 are children (and these numbers do not include an untold number of people lost under the rubble). More than 200,000 residents have been injured.

Gaza is now home to the largest cohort of child amputees in the world. Israel itself has admitted that 83 per cent, or over 51,000 of those it had killed are noncombatants, while among those it categorises as combatants are journalists, doctors, nurses, government officials and humanitarian rescuers.[31] Moreover, 86 per cent of the Gaza Strip remains within what Israel categorises as militarised zones, areas from which the population has been ordered to leave. According to the UN, at least 1.9 million people – or about 85 per cent of the population – across the Gaza Strip have been displaced during the war, many repeatedly, and some ten times or more.[32]

Israel has also ramped up its campaign of apartheid, violence and ethnic cleansing in the West Bank. More than 1,000 Palestinians, including more than 200 children, have been killed in the West Bank since October 2023 by Israeli forces and Israeli settlers. More than 9,000 people have been injured. More than 36,000 people have been displaced and more than 3,000 structures have been demolished.

The genocide did not begin in October 2023. And it did not end in October 2025. Jeff Halper, co-founder of the Israeli Committee Against House Demolitions, implored the Tribunal to understand Israel's latest actions in Gaza as an explicit step in its decades-long settler-colonial plan. 'If Israel can get rid of half the Palestinian population of the occupied territory,' Halper explained, 'then it's gone a long way again towards erasing the Palestinian presence.'

Ben Jamal, Director of Palestine Solidarity Campaign, put it best:

> I, like most of you, have witnessed this from afar. Although Palestinian, I have no family in Gaza. Indeed, no family anywhere in historic Palestine. All of my relatives were expelled in 1948 or forced into exile soon after that… History did not begin on October the 7th. That this genocide is built on the foundations of an incremental genocide decades old, 76 years of settler colonisation, occupation and apartheid and imposition across all of historic Palestine from the river to the sea.

This is the context in which witness testimony should be read, digested and understood. We now turn to that testimony, which exposes Israel's military campaign for what it is: a masterpiece of crimes against humanity.

Medicide

Since the beginning of the genocide, Israel has carried out over 750 attacks on Gaza's healthcare facilities and staff. Several thousand civilians have been killed and injured in these attacks, among them doctors, nurses, medics and ambulance drivers. About two-thirds of the hospitals are no longer operational, and those that remain open operate with limited capacity due to lack of fuel, medicine, medical equipment and food. Dialysis and cancer patients, as well as many pregnant women have nowhere to go. Many people die each day due to causes that are medically preventable. This is 'medicide': the systematic and near-total destruction of the Palestinian medical system with the aim of obliterating the conditions needed for saving and sustaining the lives of the sick and the wounded.[33]

After the Israeli imposition of a complete siege on Gaza and withdrawal of the supply of electricity to the enclave, hospitals had to make difficult decisions about who to operate on and treat.[34] By 12 October 2023, five days after the Israeli airstrikes began, hospitals risked 'turning into morgues', with thousands of Palestinian civilians and children wounded by the Israeli bombing being left untreated.[35]

Beyond the damage caused to Palestinian health care by the withdrawal of basic services, the direct targeting of Palestinian healthcare infrastructure by air attack was immediate and repeated. By 15 October, there had been 48 reported attacks on healthcare facilities in the Gaza Strip, causing damage to 24, including 6 hospitals.[36] By mid-November, the Palestinian medical system was deemed to be on the 'brink of collapse', according to various journalists and other observers, with over two-thirds of hospitals non-functional and only one hospital operating in northern Gaza.[37] UN Special Rapporteur Francesca Albanese and Maarten van der Heijden, a health lawyer, argue that these attacks often took place or were excused under the 'humanitarian camouflage' of international humanitarian law, with the Israeli government frequently claiming, without evidence, that such strikes or attacks were lawful since the hospitals were shielding combatants.[38] Nicola Perugini and Neve Gordon call this 'medical lawfare', a term they coined to describe how Israel has been justifying its systematic attacks on healthcare facilities in the Gaza Strip, mobilising the laws of armed conflict related to 'hospital shields' to securitise life-saving infrastructure and legitimise their destruction.[39]

A UN Commission of Inquiry found that by 23 December 2023, the few hospitals that remained were focusing on the treatment of conflict-related injuries.[40] Attacks on Palestinian hospitals, via ground and air, continued through 2024 and 2025, underscoring that the Palestinian medical system was purposefully wiped out by Israel.[41] The Israeli military has killed over 1,700 medical staff, targeting them at times in their homes with their families, and has taken hundreds more hostage since 7 October 2023.[42] Indeed, data indicates that healthcare workers in Gaza are three times more likely to be killed than other civilians.

Testimony from the Tribunal revealed the desperate conditions faced by the Palestinian medical staff remaining in Gaza. Reduced to performing only lifesaving surgeries in a collapsed healthcare system, even these have often been conducted under rudimentary conditions, under torchlight and with a minimum of painkillers and anaesthetics.[43]

Dr Victoria Rose, an NHS consultant plastic surgeon who has been on several medical missions to Gaza during the genocide, told the Tribunal that she operated on children daily, and described the nature of their blast injuries:

> Anything around them when the bomb went off is then whipped up and ejected at very high velocity and hits them. So, we were seeing children with bits of their body blown off.
>
> I looked at one day's operating in May and we operated on six children. We started with an eighteen-month-old child – that's not the youngest child I treated – with a 15 per cent burn. We then went on to a three-year-old boy with a 35 per cent burn… I then operated on a five-year-old girl who had had her arm blown off. She was down for an amputation, but we managed to salvage half of her hand and most of her forearm and shoulder. I then operated on her sister whilst my colleagues operated on her mother in the theatre next door. Her sister had had her left cheek and shoulder blown off. I then operated on a seven-year-old girl who had had her knee blown off. And my final case was a thirteen-year-old boy who had had his left ankle blown off and his brother was being operated in the theatre next door.

Dr Rose further described in harrowing detail the impact of Israel's restrictions on medical equipment:

> When we were there, we ran out of analgesia, which meant that, unlike in the UK when we amputate your leg, we'll give you some anaesthesia, some local anaesthetic into the

stump so that you don't wake up in pain. We were not able to do that. So, every day that I operated, the first six cases would be children and the screaming in the recovery room would not stop until about three in the afternoon and we had no analgesia to give those children. We also ran out of antibiotics. We had two types left, neither of which would be indicated [for use] in dirty open war wounds. We ran out of disinfectant solutions, which we ended up having to water down, and we ran out of scalpel blades, which we ended up having to re-sterilise.

Patients were also suffering from immunosuppression, as an effect of malnutrition caused by Israel's blockade on humanitarian aid. This led to a sharp rise in preventable illnesses and gravely impacted the health of the medical staff:

> Obviously the malnutrition is very evident now in the images that are getting out. I think we really noticed it in our colleagues initially. All of the team that I went with lost weight. I lost half a stone in twenty-eight days. I didn't see any fresh fruit or vegetables. I only ate the food that I took in with me. There was nothing else available.

Professor Nick Maynard, who treated several patients in Gaza during the genocide, told the Tribunal that 'the infrastructure of the whole healthcare system has been nearly totally destroyed'. He described the conditions faced by medical staff in Gaza:

> The Israeli military went into the hospital. They dismantled the whole infrastructure of the hospital. They destroyed the scanning machines. They cut the cables to all the ultrasound machines. They cut the cables and destroyed all

> the dialysis machines. … The Israeli military bombed the intensive care unit whilst I was operating in the operating theatre next door…
>
> Healthcare workers have been directly targeted. More than 1,600 healthcare workers have been killed. More than 450 have been abducted, illegally detained, tortured. Many of them have been killed, including close friends of mine.
>
> We were operating with virtually no resources in the operating theatre. Often no water to use to scrub up to sterilise our hands and the equipment. Often no sterile drapes or sterile gloves because no aid has been allowed into Gaza. No painkillers.

Since the so-called ceasefire, severe shortages of medical supplies have remained.[44] No plans have been made to rebuild Gaza's ravaged health system, a situation compounded by new and politicised restrictions on aid groups' access to Gaza.[45] Thirty-seven aid groups have been blocked from accessing Gaza under the new criteria, further depriving medical centres of supplies and support for their operations at a time when over 18,000 patients are in need of urgent medical evacuation.[46]

In the time that he had, Professor Maynard told the Tribunal about several of the patients he treated at Al-Aqsa Hospital.

> Let me tell you about Ali and Aya, a brother and a sister who I treated in Al-Aqsa last year. They were the sole remaining members of their family. Their parents and their siblings had all been killed by a bomb that bombed their tent in Al-Mawasi, the so-called safe area, we're told by the Israeli propaganda. Ali had a severe chest injury. Aya had

> a severe leg injury. We had to treat both of them without any pain relief at all... I can still hear their screams as we treated them without any anaesthetic at all.

He also remembered a young girl named Nada.

> [Nada] came in 3 hours after Ali and had burns that were so severe she wasn't going to survive. She wouldn't have survived in London, in Oxford, let alone Gaza. You could see her facial bones because the flesh was burnt so badly. She died an agonising death on the floor of the waiting area of the emergency room in pain because we had no pain relief to give her.

Dr Natalie Roberts, executive director of Doctors Without Borders, UK (Médecins Sans Frontières [MSF UK]), provided more evidence of the targeting of healthcare and humanitarian workers. Several of her colleagues were killed. One, Reem Abu Lebdeh, was a physiotherapist who was killed alongside her parents and siblings in their house in December 2023 when the area came under a massive Israeli ground and air assault. The bodies of her mother and sister were eventually recovered from the rubble in February 2024, but Reem's body has never been found. At the time of Dr Roberts's testimony, Reem was one of twelve Palestinian MSF colleagues who had been killed by Israeli forces in Gaza since October 2023.

Dr Mahmoud Abu Nujaila and Dr Ahmad Al Sahar were two MSF doctors working in Al-Awda Hospital. They were killed when the hospital was hit by an Israeli strike on 21 November 2023. Their colleague Alaa Al-Shawa, a nurse, was killed on 18 November 2023, when a clearly marked MSF convoy came under attack from Israeli forces in Gaza City, despite having authorisation to evacuate the area. Alaa was shot in the head. The MSF team tried to stop the bleeding, but they were unable to save his life.

Dr Roberts also testified that Israeli raids on hospitals resulted in the arbitrary detention, torture and forced disappearances of MSF staff. On 26 October 2024, during a raid on Kamal Adwan Hospital, MSF surgeon Muhammad Obeid was arrested with 57 others. He is currently held in an Israeli prison. No formal charges have been brought against him.

'Medical staff seem to be systematically targeted as one element of the deliberate dismantling of the health system in Gaza,' Dr Roberts told the Tribunal. 'Our medical teams are working under the harshest of conditions with little food for themselves while they're watching patients die due to the Israeli blockade and bombardment.' Describing how her MSF colleagues had been displaced multiple times, Dr Roberts quoted her colleague, Dr Muhammed Abu Mughaisseeb:

> Before she died, my mother told me death can sometimes be a relief. I didn't understand her at the time, but today, after all I've been through, I do. Displacement is harder than death. I've been forced from my home, stripped of safety, carrying my bag from one destroyed place to another. We endure hunger that eats our bodies, and a constant fear that drains our minds, and a psychological stress that never stops. It follows us in every breath, every thought, every sound of the night. And then there are the missiles and bombs. The roar as they pass overhead. The whistle tearing through my sky. The dreadful silence before they strike. Leaving me to wonder, is it my turn now? Now I know what my mother meant. Death may bring peace, but what I live through, this hunger, this endless fear, this unrelenting stress is a pain far beyond death.

'In summary,' Dr Roberts told the Tribunal, 'I stand by our position that MSF teams in Gaza are witnessing war crimes, crimes against humanity and genocide according to the definition laid out in the Genocide Convention.'

The damage Israel caused to the Gazan health system has decimated the infrastructure necessary to provide basic access to health care. MSF have described the destruction of the Palestinian health system as a form collective punishment, while both the UN Commission of Inquiry and Physicians for Human Rights, Israel, have deemed the 'deliberate and systematic dismantling of Gaza's health and life-sustaining systems' met the legal definition of genocide.[47] The UN has noted especially the obliteration of reproductive healthcare centres in Gaza, which represents an attempt to destroy the future of the Palestinian people.[48]

Let us see the provision of health care for what it is: a mode of governance that plays a crucial role in resisting the occupation of Palestine and the dehumanisation of its people. Israel aims to render Gaza ungovernable; by depriving Palestinians of the ability to provide health care, Israel threatens to erode their moral resilience against injustice.[49] But that moral resilience will never be destroyed.

Scholasticide

Educational institutions were not spared from Israeli military attack, reflecting a policy that is based on the view that the 'entire [Palestinian] nation' was responsible for the war crimes that took place on 7 October 2023.[50] The United Nations recorded more than 200 attacks on schools in Gaza by 24 March 2024, with 53 of these schools being totally destroyed.[51] Nearly three months later, by June 2024, 76 per cent of schools required 'full reconstruction or major rehabilitation', and by August 2024, 85 per cent of Gaza's 737 schools had been destroyed or damaged by Israeli attacks.[52] May 2025 marked a peak in Israeli violence against the Palestinian education system. By this time, 95.5 per cent of institutions had been damaged or destroyed.[53]

By April 2024, six months into Israel's attacks, already 261 teachers had been killed and 756 injured, while at the time of writing the number of teachers and other educational staff who have been killed has risen to at least 782.[54] Repeatedly, schools have been struck by attacks from the air, in many cases after they had been converted into shelters for displaced Palestinians.[55]

Higher education has also been targeted. By July 2024, all 19 universities in Gaza had suffered severe damage, with 80 per cent of university buildings destroyed and 90,000 students prevented from carrying on their studies.[56] At least 105 academics have been killed, many purposefully, decimating a source of future learning for the Palestinian people.[57]

The damage to primary, secondary and higher education has severely curtailed the prospects of young Palestinians who are unable to continue their education – approximately 625,000 young people, according to recent estimates.[58] The Gaza People's Tribunal (another civil society led initiative, held in Sarajevo and Istanbul in May and October 2025) and others have termed this a scholasticide: the destruction of Palestine's intellectual future through the elimination of a generation of teachers, students and their educational institutions.[59]

There has been an almost ritualistic element in this violence against educational institutions. Israeli soldiers have been recorded cheering at the destruction of UNRWA schools, while it also appears relatively commonplace for Israeli troops to film or photograph themselves vandalising schools and burning libraries.[60] The most prominent example of this trend occurred at the Israa University, which was destroyed via controlled demolition on 18 January 2024. The University had previously been converted into military barracks by the Israeli military and had served as such for 70 days until its final (and filmed) destruction.[61]

These brazen attacks on educational infrastructure have wiped out generations of Palestinian cultural presence. Dr Ahmed Alhussaina, the vice-president of Israa University, noted that thousands of pre-Islamic, Islamic and Roman artefacts were destroyed or looted from the university, eradicating the ability of Palestinians to speak of their own history, heritage and cultural memory.[62] With the destruction of the other 18 universities across Gaza, the Palestinian presence in history is further erased.[63]

Raphael Lemkin has defined genocide as a 'coordinated plan of different actions aiming at the destruction of essential foundations of the life of national groups, with the aim of annihilating the groups themselves'.[64] The obliteration of Palestinian schools and universities aims to destroy Palestinian prosperity, culture and the potential of future generations to place themselves in history. It can be termed nothing other than genocidal, a policy that seeks to disintegrate the sentiment that binds together the Palestinian nation; while the material Palestinian nation is destroyed in hails of bombs and missile strikes.[65]

Journalism's graveyard

Israel has killed over 250 Palestinian journalists since 7 October 2023. This briefly attracted international attention after it was calculated that more journalists have died in Gaza than in the US Civil War, First and Second World Wars, the Korean War, the Vietnam War, the wars in Yugoslavia in the 1990s and 2000s, and the post-9/11 war in Afghanistan combined.[66]

As part of its effort to eliminate witnesses and control the narrative, Israel has, as one commentator wrote, transformed Gaza into journalism's graveyard.[67] Within a month of the onslaught, the Israeli military had destroyed most of the news agencies and media institutions in Gaza in a calculated effort to silence independent reporting. As part of this campaign, Israel targeted Gaza's connectivity, destroying over 50 per cent of Gaza's telecommunications infrastructure and damaging an additional 25 per cent. Israel's bombing spree hit local and international media organisations alike, across all parts of the media ecosystem: radio and TV stations, press offices, transmission towers, and media institutions, internet cables, and live camera positions broadcasting the military offensive. At the time of writing, Israel had destroyed or damaged 112 governmental and non-governmental media institutions, including 15 news agency headquarters, 21 radio stations, 15 satellite channels, 3 broadcast towers, 6 newspapers, and 13 institutions providing media and journalistic services.

Concurrently, a pattern of threats and attacks on journalists working for local and international news outlets emerged. Israel created target banks of journalists and circulated 'kill lists', falsely accusing journalists of being Hamas combatants. They and their families were threatened, and often those killed were killed alongside their families in their homes or tents. Many others were killed walking on the streets or driving on roads. From October 2023 to April 2026, the Israeli army killed over 250 journalists, more than any country on record.

Palestinian journalists have operated in conditions marked not only by generalised danger, but by what multiple journalists describe as a deliberate pattern of targeting and intimidation because of their professional role. Journalists on the ground have consistently characterised themselves as simultaneously witnesses to events and direct targets of harm.[68]

Journalist Abubaker Abed told the Tribunal that during his work in Gaza, he was directly threatened by Israeli forces, and was subject to coordinated harassment on social media by accounts portraying journalists as legitimate military targets. According to Abed, such narratives are used to justify attacks on journalists by alleging covert or improper activity, despite the reality that Gaza-based reporters are engaged in continuous, visible and time-sensitive documentation work that leaves no plausible basis for claims of 'secret' terrorism. In parallel, multiple international press-freedom monitors and United Nations actors have described Gaza as an exceptionally dangerous environment for media workers, with unusually high levels of journalist fatalities and injuries reported over the course of the conflict. Separate reporting that cites the International Federation of Journalists similarly placed Gaza among the deadliest contexts for press workers, while noting Israel's positioning of journalists as press combatants.[69]

Journalists in Gaza have repeatedly sought protection from international media organisations and press-freedom bodies – overwhelmingly in vain. In his account, Abed states that this absence of meaningful protection or accountability has reinforced the perception that journalists are exposed without recourse, even as fatalities mount. He describes a moment in which threats against him caused acute fear for his family's safety, crystallising in the realisation that neither international institutions nor media employers would intervene to protect Palestinian journalists. He frames this experience as emblematic of what has occurred to hundreds of journalists, whom he believes have been deliberately targeted in part because they have been publicly framed as a threat.

In addition to physical danger, Abed describes professional mistreatment by international media outlets, including instances in which journalists were commissioned for work but not paid, or had their bylines removed from articles or segments they worked on without explanation. He characterises these practices as efforts by international outlets to shield themselves from political pressure, at the expense of the safety, livelihood and professional recognition of Palestinian journalists. In his assessment, the failure of Western media institutions to report fully or to defend their local journalists has materially contributed to continued violence, by limiting scrutiny and normalising the silencing of those documenting events on the ground.

Beyond the overall scale of casualties, press-freedom organisations and UN experts have raised concern about the recurrence of incidents in which journalists were harmed during or shortly after strikes, including circumstances giving rise to allegations of unlawful targeting, reckless disregard or failure to take feasible precautions.[70] Moreover, several incidents referenced by the UN illustrate the acute dangers faced by journalists even when operating near civilian sites, for example, near Nasser Hospital in Gaza.[71]

Tareq Abu Azzoum, who described Gaza as 'the laboratory

of collective punishment', told the Tribunal that Palestinian journalists occupy a uniquely perilous role: they are not only documenting the genocide but living through it. He recounted that numerous journalists have been killed while actively reporting in the field, including while sheltering with their families in temporary refuges. These deaths, he emphasises, underscore that journalists are not merely exposed to incidental risk but are being deliberately and systematically targeted and, on several occasions, killed alongside their families. Indeed, 700 family members of Palestinian journalists have been killed.

Abu Azzoum further linked the danger faced by Palestinian journalists to the near-total absence of international media outlets operating independently inside Gaza. He characterises this prohibition set by Israel as striving to create conditions in which the full reality of events is obscured. In his account, the sustained reliance on local journalists, combined with severe technical and logistical obstacles alongside their systematic exposure to harm, reflects a method by which the flow of information, and, indeed, evidence, is constrained: when those who document events are killed, threatened or discredited, the public record itself is imperilled.

UN experts have publicly linked the multiple killings of journalists to the risk of eliminating independent documentation, warning that continued losses may result in journalists being silenced as a class of witnesses.[72]

Taken together, these accounts contribute to a broader evidentiary picture in which Palestinian journalists in Gaza are subjected to threats, lethal violence, professional marginalisation and institutional abandonment, all in connection with their role in documenting the violence and providing evidence of atrocity crimes. The cumulative effect, as described by journalists themselves, is not only the loss of life and safety, but the erosion of independent reporting and the suppression of evidence. Israel's assault on journalists is an assault on press freedom, civilian protection and the preservation of truth.

Starvation

Since early 2025, conditions in Gaza have evolved from chronic food insecurity into what humanitarian actors describe as a manufactured famine, driven not by natural scarcity but by the deliberate destruction of agricultural lands, greenhouses and irrigation infrastructure – all vital sources of food.[73] Forensic Architecture, a group that uses forensic tools to investigate human rights violations, says that 'the destruction of agricultural land and infrastructure in Gaza is a deliberate act of ecocide'.[74]

Already in the early months of Israel's onslaught, large swathes of land were razed by soldiers using D9 bulldozers and explosives to expand the 'buffer zone' on Gaza's side of the border from 300 metres to an estimated 500–800 metres. Israeli naval forces have also damaged or destroyed around 70 per cent of Gaza's fishing vessels. Driven by hunger, a few fishermen still go out to sea in small vessels, risking the wrath of naval forces; some of them have been attacked and killed, as the fishermen's association in Gaza reports.[75]

Simultaneously, Israel has imposed sustained restrictions on the entry and quantity of food. This includes a concerted campaign to criminalise and eliminate the United Nations Relief and Works Agency (UNRWA), by far the largest distributor of food in the Gaza Strip. Humanitarian workers, medical professionals and international agencies have consistently warned that starvation in Gaza is the foreseeable result of policy decisions governing access, rather than an unintended byproduct of conflict.[76]

Humanitarian worker Hala Sabbah told the Tribunal that from 2 March to 19 May 2025, the entry of aid and commercial trucks into Gaza effectively ceased. According to her account, trucks stopped entering for an extended period, severing access to food supplies even for aid groups attempting mass distribution. She linked this cut-off directly to the widespread images documented in June and July 2025 of children dying from starvation, explaining that mutual aid networks were unable to locate food in local markets because none was available to purchase. This period coincided with warnings from UN agencies that Gaza was entering the most severe phase of food deprivation seen during the conflict.[77] Sabbah contextualised this collapse by contrasting it with pre-war conditions. During the 17-year blockade prior to October 2023, approximately 500 trucks per day were permitted to enter Gaza. While insufficient to meet full nutritional needs, this volume allowed the population to survive at a subsistence level, even as already then there had been documentation of malnutrition among segments of the population. By contrast, current access has been reduced to approximately 75 to 85 trucks every few days, a fraction of what is required for a population exceeding 2 million people.

This account mirrors assessments by humanitarian bodies that the volume of aid entering Gaza falls far below minimum survival thresholds.[78] Beyond the drastic reduction in quantity, Sabbah emphasised that the composition of permitted aid has been tightly controlled. According to her account, trucks are restricted to a narrow range of staples, primarily rice, lentils and flour, while foods essential for addressing acute malnutrition are systematically excluded. Medical and nutrition experts have repeatedly warned that such diets are incapable of reversing severe malnutrition, particularly among children, pregnant women and the elderly. International health agencies have similarly cautioned that prolonged reliance on nutritionally incomplete food accelerates wasting, stunting and immune collapse, even when minimal caloric intake is maintained.

Professor Nick Maynard saw the effects of man-made famine first hand while treating patients at Nasser Hospital. Zainab was just seven months old when she was admitted. 'She looked like a newborn. You could see every rib, every bone in her body… There was not a single bottle of formula feed. She died whilst I was there.' Maynard described how just four days before, a group of US doctors had attempted to bring in formula feed, but every bottle was confiscated by the Israeli border guards.

Professor Maynard also described a patient he had treated at Nasser Hospital just a few weeks before his appearance at the Tribunal.

> Let me tell you about Habiba, a beautiful eleven-year-old girl who I spent the whole night operating on one night. She had a bad chest injury … I had to spend the whole night reconstructing her oesophagus which had been destroyed by the explosive injury. We couldn't feed her afterwards. She died four weeks later because we couldn't get any feed to feed her. And that feed could have saved her if it had been allowed in by the Israelis and they had stopped that feed coming in.

The human consequences of the blockade were most acute in late July and early August 2025.[79] During this period, humanitarian workers themselves were operating under extreme conditions, with temperatures exceeding 35 degrees Celsius, while attempting to erect tents, search for food and provide assistance across displacement camps. Sabbah reported that team members fainted from hunger and exhaustion while working, requiring intravenous fluids and nutritional supplements simply to continue their duties. These accounts align with broader reporting that humanitarian responders in Gaza have been forced to operate while themselves being malnourished. During this time, Sabbah said, community kitchens ceased operating for approximately two weeks, dramatically intensifying hunger. Community kitchens have functioned as one of the last remaining food sources for displaced populations, and their temporary collapse removed even minimal daily sustenance. When limited supplies of rice and lentils later resumed, some kitchens reopened; however, the portions they provided remained extremely inadequate. As Sabbah describes it, a 'community kitchen' meal often consisted of a single pot of lentil soup shared among families of ten to twelve people, serving as their sole food for the entire day. Humanitarian agencies have characterised such rations as far below emergency nutrition standards and insufficient to prevent death from starvation.

This pattern – severe restriction of aid volume, deliberate limitation of nutritional diversity, prolonged suspension of food entry, and the collapse of community kitchens – has been repeatedly identified by UN bodies and humanitarian organisations as creating famine conditions. UN experts have warned that when starvation results from policies that obstruct access to food, water and humanitarian relief, it constitutes not merely a humanitarian failure but a grave breach of international norms protecting civilian survival. Taken together, the testimony of humanitarian workers such as Sabbah, corroborated by international reporting and agency assessments, demonstrates that famine in Gaza has not emerged spontaneously. Rather, it has been produced through sustained control over food access, rendering starvation predictable, widespread and lethal.

Pedro Arrojo-Agudo, the UN Special Rapporteur on the human right to safe drinking water and sanitation, told the Tribunal that even before October 2023, the Gaza Strip's drinking water supply met only the needs of around 50 per cent of the population. Following Israel's military operations in Gaza, 90 per cent of water and sanitation facilities – including water wells, irrigation, dissemination units and treatment facilities – have been destroyed and or damaged by bombing or blasting. Pedro Arrojo-Agudo told the Tribunal that Israel was 'using water as a weapon of war in clear violation of the fourth Geneva Convention'.[80] Arrojo-Agudo received numerous reports of deliberate attacks against water personnel and humanitarian workers. In February 2024, Israel confirmed that its troops were flooding underground tunnels with sea water, causing catastrophic damage to Gaza's groundwater, upon which the strip's 2.3 million people largely depend.

Arrojo-Agudo also described the crisis in sanitation. In November 2023, in some of the most crowded shelters in the south of Gaza, there was only one toilet per 600 internally displaced persons, making open defecation the only option.

On displacement more generally, we heard from Paula Gavira Betanur, UN Special Rapporteur on the human rights of internally displaced persons. She told the Tribunal that almost 2 million Palestinians have been forced from their homes since October 2023. 'Let it be clear,' she said, 'this is not evacuation for safety,' but part of 'a systematic attempt to dismantle civilian life' and 'an attempt to push Palestinians from their homeland, not to protect them within it.'

Women and girls have borne a disproportionately heavy burden of the sanitation crisis. Arrojo-Agudo explained that tens of thousands of women have given birth 'in the midst of this hell', in inhumane conditions and without the means to feed their babies. It is estimated that, as of May 2025, there were more than 55,000 pregnant women in Gaza.[81] The most serious problem was the contamination of water. This contributed to more than 70,000 cases of diarrhoea per week in children under the age of five.

'All these actions pursued by Israel,' Arrojo-Agudo concluded, 'could amount to a pattern of conduct deliberately inflicting [severe damage] on the group's condition of life, calculated to bring about its physical destruction.' These actions, he said, violate the occupying powers' obligations under Article 56 of the Fourth Geneva Convention. Arrojo-Agudo reminded the Tribunal that deprivation of food access, including drinking water and medicine, is a crime against humanity clearly defined in the Rome Statute; and that Article II of the Genocide Convention prohibits acts committed with intent to destroy in whole or in part a national, ethnical, racial or religious group. 'Every day we witness… evidence substantiating the essence of a genocide that we cannot ignore.'

Dr Natalie Roberts from MSF dedicated part of her testimony to the Israeli and US-led militarised food distribution system known as the Gaza Humanitarian Foundation (GHF). 'There is nothing humanitarian about the GHF,' Dr Roberts said, describing it as 'a new method of orchestrating the mass killing of Palestinians'. After Israel shut down UNRWA's 400 food distribution sites, GHF opened four sites to serve over 2 million people. These sites, Dr Roberts described, saw extreme levels of violence and led to the killing of Palestinian men, women and children who went to the sites in the hope of receiving food only to come under fire from Israeli soldiers. On 31 July 2025, the Office of the United Nations High Commissioner for Human Rights had reported that at least 1,373 Palestinian aid seekers were killed: 859 near GHF's sites and 514 near UN and other organisations' aid convoys. The Ministry of Health in Gaza reported that more than 7,200 people were injured while attempting to collect aid in sites that became death traps. Dr Roberts recalled how MSF medical teams would treat people with gunshot wounds, barbed wire lacerations and crush injuries sustained while trying to receive food at these GHF distribution sites. One victim was Dr Roberts's colleague, Abdullah Hammed, who was killed by Israeli forces on 3 July 2025, as he waited to collect flour from a truck.

Professor Nick Maynard also operated on patients who had been targeted at these sites. He described to the Tribunal how, during his last trip to Gaza, he had spent most days operating on young teenage boys who had been shot by Israeli soldiers at the food distribution points. 'Not only were they being shot,' he said 'but there was clear evidence of targeting of specific body parts on particular days.' He continued:

> One day, 19 young teenage boys were admitted to the ER, all of whom had been shot in the head or neck. The next day, they came in having been shot in the chest. The next day, the abdomen. The day after that, the legs. On one day at the beginning of my final week at Nasser Hospital, four young teenage boys were brought in. This clustering of

> injuries to particular body parts was beyond coincidence. It was clear evidence of target practice by the Israeli soldiers on these young teenage boys.

Construction is destruction

Eyal Weizman from Forensic Architecture delivered a visual presentation of the scale of destruction in Gaza, or what he called 'ungrounding'. More than mere 'destruction', ungrounding is 'the erasure of everything on the surface' – a level of devastation that was 'different than any other form of destruction that Forensic Architecture has seen over the years'. As Weizman explained, Israel carried out similar 'ungrounding' throughout the Nakba of 1948. In both cases, the destruction was part of the settler-colonial project, motivated by efforts to ethnically cleanse the Palestinians through the 'shrinking of the living space'.

The most harrowing part of Weizman's testimony was the description of destroyed buildings as 'mass graves'. Many thousands of Palestinians have not been recovered, and their bodies have been left in the rubble. Some of that rubble is being recycled as building material. This material is being piled up to create infrastructure for the Israeli army, barriers, bases and detention facilities where Palestinian men are being tortured. 'All this architecture is made out of this rubble' – rubble that contains the unrecovered bodies of Palestinian people.

As Weizman explained, Israel's aim is 'to redesign by destruction'. In other words, construction *is* destruction. 'Gaza is both a demolition zone, active systematic demolition of all traces of Palestinian life and a construction site.' This is the context in which we must understand the Western-backed 'reconstruction' plans in Gaza, which Weizman described as 'the continuation of genocide by other means'.

Three days before the Gaza Tribunal was held, the *Washington Post* published a 38-page slide deck of US President Donald Trump's plans to take over the Gaza Strip, resettle its population and turn the swathe of land into 'the Riviera of the Middle East'.[82] Among the proposals were AI-powered 'smart cities', and a manufacturing hub named after Elon Musk. Palestinians would be encouraged into 'voluntary' resettlement, either to another country or into restricted zones. Palestinians who own land would be given 'digital tokens' to support a new life elsewhere. Using large-scale ethnic cleansing as a real-estate opportunity, Trump's proposals were developed by some of the same people who created the deadly 'Gaza Humanitarian Foundation'. Later that month, Donald Trump said Tony Blair wished to join the US President's 'Board of Peace', tasked with occupying Gaza if a ceasefire was reached. In January 2026, Blair was named on the Board alongside Marco Rubio, Jared Kushner and others. Also invited to join were Vladamir Putin and Benjamin Netanyahu.

One of the council members of the so-called Board of Peace is Liran Tancman, one of the five founders of the deadly Gaza Humanitarian Foundation.

Home by home

'It is the most fatal conflict for civilians that we have ever documented,' Emily Tripp, the executive director of Airwars explained, adding that: 'These records tell us that by every metric, the level of civilian harm in Gaza is simply incomparable with any twenty-first century air campaign.' Airwars documents civilian harm in war zones, and to date has published detailed incident reports outlining where and how more than 10,000 civilians have been killed in Gaza. 'We have names. We have ages. We have professions. We know whether they were at home [or] sheltering in schools, whether they're in an ambulance with their families in hospitals, whether they were trying to find food at an aid distribution,' she elaborated. Tripp also told the Tribunal that in nine out of ten incidents where women were killed, they were killed alongside a child. On average, when civilians were killed alongside family members, they were killed alongside at least 15 of their relatives. 'This is not like anything we've documented before,' she said. Home by home, hospital by hospital, generation by generation; this was no war; this was a genocide, aimed at destroying an entire people.

4

Preventing Genocide

As a permanent member of the UN Security Council, a High Contracting Party to the 1949 Geneva Conventions, a party to the Genocide Convention and the Rome Statute of the International Criminal Court, and a state with long-standing diplomatic, military and economic ties to Israel, the United Kingdom has heightened responsibilities in relation to Israel's conduct in Gaza and the wider Occupied Palestinian Territory (OPT).

These are not just political responsibilities. These are also legal duties and obligations arising under treaty law, customary international law and peremptory norms. The UK has a particular onus to respect the law given its capacity to influence events and other state actors, while its obligations were sharpened by the ICJ's January and March 2024 provisional measures, which places states on notice of a plausible risk of genocide in Gaza, and the Court's July 2024 ruling on the illegality of Israel's occupation and the decision that it must immediately withdraw from the OPT.[83]

This chapter sets out the legal duties placed upon the UK, before outlining how the UK can – and should – tangibly fulfil them.

The sources of the UK's obligations

The UK's international obligations arise from the treaties it has signed and from customary international law.[84] Responsibility extends to all organs of the government, including ministers, the armed forces and intelligence agencies. Beyond bilateral and multilateral duties, certain obligations are owed *erga omnes* (meaning, to the international community as a whole, including according to the basic rules protecting peoples' right to self-determination and the fundamental prohibitions underpinning international humanitarian law and genocide prevention).[85] Where such obligations are at stake, third states do not have discretion to treat compliance as optional.

In this context, five bodies of law are central to the UK's responsibilities:

First is the Geneva Conventions (1949). As a High Contracting Party, the UK is bound by Common Article 1 to 'respect and ensure respect' for international humanitarian law (IHL), which prohibits targeting civilians and civilian sites, collective punishment, unlawful displacement and denial of humanitarian relief.[86]

Second, the Genocide Convention (1948) obliges Britain to prevent and punish genocide.[87] This duty is proactive and extends beyond its territory, requiring action wherever the risk of genocide exists. This duty was triggered by the provisional measures of the ICJ in *South Africa* v *Israel*, January 2024.

Third, there is the Rome Statute of the International Criminal Court (ICC) (1998). As a state party, the UK must cooperate fully with the ICC, including executing arrest warrants for individuals suspected of crimes in Gaza, and must refrain from conduct that frustrates the Court's mandate.[88]

Fourth, there are a range of customary rules of state responsibility.[89] These are articulated by the International Law Commission's Draft Articles on Responsibility of States for Internationally Wrongful Acts (ARSIWA) (2001), with a focus on obligations owed towards all (namely, with *erga omnes* character). Such obligations stem from violations of *jus cogens* norms including the right to self-determination, the prohibition against racial discrimination and apartheid, and the prohibition against annexation through force. These duties were ascertained again by the ICJ in its Advisory Opinion of 19 July 2024 in Legal Consequences Arising from the Policies and Practices of Israel in the Occupied Palestinian Territory, including East Jerusalem.

Finally, Britain is bound by its own domestic legislation, including the International Criminal Court Act 2001 and export control laws, which require it to criminalise and prevent grave international crimes and to deny arms transfers where there's a real risk of misuse.

The ICJ: Genocide

In December 2023, South Africa took an historic step and instituted proceedings against Israel at the International Court of Justice, the highest court in the land.[90] South Africa alleged that Israel was committing genocide against the Palestinian people, stating that 'acts and omissions' by Israel were 'genocidal in character because they are intended to bring about the destruction of a substantial part of the Palestinian national, racial and ethnical group'. They cited statements from Israeli government officials, including Prime Minister

Benjamin Netanyahu, as evidence of 'genocidal intent'. On this basis, South Africa requested that the ICJ take 'provisional measures' in order to prevent 'imminent and irreparable loss' of lives in Gaza.

The Court ruled on the provisional measures request on 26 January 2024. The ICJ found that 'at least some of the rights claimed by South Africa and for which it is seeking protection are plausible'. This included 'the right of the Palestinians in Gaza to be protected from acts of genocide and related prohibited acts identified in Article 3 of the Genocide Convention, and the right of South Africa to seek Israel's compliance with the latter's obligations under the Convention'. The ICJ ruled that there was a real and imminent risk of irreparable prejudice to those rights.

The order placed all states on clear notice that their duty to prevent genocide is engaged. This obligation flows directly from Article 1 of the Genocide Convention, which requires States to undertake measures 'to prevent and to punish genocide'. Invoking the *Bosnia* v *Serbia* case, the ICJ clarified that these obligations become active once 'its organs were aware that genocide was about to be committed or was under way, and if the aid and assistance supplied, from the moment they became so aware onwards, to the perpetrators of the criminal acts… enabled or facilitated the commission of the acts'.[91]

In other words, the duty to prevent genocide begins the moment that a state becomes aware of the existence of a serious risk that genocide may be committed. The ICJ's ruling stated that 'a real and imminent risk that irreparable prejudice will be caused to the rights found by the Court to be plausible'. From this moment, then, the UK could no longer claim that it was not aware of the risk of genocide. By the time the Gaza

Tribunal was held, more than 19 months had passed since this ruling was handed down.

The UK's obligations under the Geneva Convention were further highlighted two months after the initial ruling when the ICJ issued a second round of provisional measures. On 28 March 2024, the Court ordered intensified actions to prevent genocide in Gaza, calling on Israel to ensure unhindered, large-scale aid and to prevent military actions violating the Genocide Convention.

During their witness testimony at the Tribunal, both the Special Rapporteur on the situation of human rights in the Palestinian territory occupied since 1967, Francesca Albanese and Tayab Ali, the Director of International Centre of Justice for Palestinians (ICJP), urged people not to downplay the significance of International Court of Justice's provisional measures. 'The only reason a court issues provisional orders is if it's trying to prevent something,' Ali said, 'and it only tries to prevent something if it thinks something is going to happen or is happening or is likely to happen.'

As both Ali and Albanese emphasised, the ICJ did not just order *Israel* to take specific actions in order to prevent irreparable harm to the Palestinian people. The ICJ ruling also had clear implications for third-party states, including the UK. 'At that precise moment,' Ali said, 'every state, including Britain, had a binding duty to prevent genocide.' This duty 'arises the instant a state knows or should know of a serious risk'.

This was echoed by Dr Gearóid Ó Cuinn, of the Global Legal Action Network (GLAN). 'There is a legal consensus that the UK's duty to prevent genocide was crystallised [following the January 2024 ICJ ruling] in respect of Israel's offensive in Gaza,' he said. 'This duty requires the UK to take all reasonably available measures within its power which might contribute to the prevention of genocide.' This duty, he concluded, is 'the beating heart of the Genocide Convention, the legal expression of "never again"'.

The ICJ: Illegal occupation

Since October 2023, Israel's genocidal acts have been migrating from the Gaza Strip to the West Bank. In August 2025, Israeli Finance Minister Bezalel Smotrich announced plans to implement the so-called 'E1' project. Releasing a statement headlined 'Burying the idea of a Palestinian state', a spokesperson for Smotrich confirmed that 3,000 homes would be built in the occupied West Bank, creating a wedge between the north and south. 'There is nothing to recognise and no one to recognise,' Smotrich said. 'Anyone in the world who tries today to recognise a Palestinian state will receive an answer from us on the ground.'

Indeed. Over the past two and a half years, Israel has accelerated settlement expansion and annexation of large parts of the occupied West Bank. In the year leading up to October 2025, more than 36,000 Palestinians were displaced. There were more than 1,700 incidents of settler violence resulting in deaths, injury and whole communities being displaced from their villages. During that time, Israeli authorities approved 36,973 housing units in occupied East Jerusalem and 27,200 in the rest of the West Bank.

In March 2025, *No Other Land*, a film about Palestinians fighting to protect their homes from demolition by Israel, won an Oscar for Best Documentary Feature. Just weeks later, one of the film's co-directors, Hamdan Ballal, was attacked by Israeli settlers and detained by the Israeli military. Ballal described it as the 'worst moment' of his life. Four months later, one of the documentary's contributors, Odeh Hadalin, was shot and killed by an Israeli settler. 'Odeh just died. Murdered,' wrote the film's other co-director, Yuval Abraham.

Smotrich's announcement and Hadalin's murder were both preceded by a landmark ruling by the ICJ. On 19 July 2024, the ICJ concluded that Israel's very presence in the OPT (Gaza, the West Bank and East Jerusalem) was illegal, involving breaches of the Fourth Geneva Convention, as well as peremptory norms including the Palestinian people's right to self-determination, the prohibition on acquisition of territory by force, and the prohibition of apartheid and racial segregation.[92] The court found that, irrespective of the specific violations Israel carries out within these territories, its mere presence in Gaza, the West Bank and East Jerusalem over such an extended period violates the prohibition on racial segregation and apartheid under international law. More specifically, the Court found that Israel has violated a number of peremptory (*jus cogens*) norms, including the right of self-determination, the basic norms of international humanitarian law, the prohibition against racial discrimination and apartheid, and the prohibition on annexation. *Jus cogens* norms are hierarchical compared to other norms of international law, and their violation sets in motion obligations for all states.

The ICJ concluded that Israel's very presence in the occupied Palestinian territories is illegal and is sustained only through the ongoing use of force – constituting an act of aggression of a continuing character. The Court's unambiguous finding authoritatively ascertains that Israel's presence in the OPT must end 'as *rapidly as possible*'.[93]

During his testimony, Tayab Ali clarified what it means for a Court to offer an 'Advisory Opinion'. This is not 'advice you can take or leave,' he said. Instead, it means that the ICJ has been asked to determine the settled position in international law about a situation. The ICJ is advising on what that position is – and it is an opinion 'telling you what your obligations are'.

The landmark opinion did not only lay out obligations for Israel, but for third states too. The Court reaffirmed that third states have interlocking duties of (i) non-recognition, (ii) non-assistance, and (iii) cooperation to bring the unlawful situation to an end. The obligation of non-assistance, the Court stated, entails a duty 'not to render aid or assistance in maintaining the situation created by Israel's illegal presence in the OPT'.

The Court's declaration reaffirmed principles pertaining to *erga omnes* (owed to all) obligations grounded in customary international law. 'Among the obligations *erga omnes* violated by Israel are the obligation to respect the right of the Palestinian people to self-determination and the obligation arising from the prohibition of the use of force to acquire territory as well as certain of its obligations under international humanitarian law and international human rights law,' the Justices explained. They also stressed the responsibilities of third-state parties as outlined in the International Law Commission's Draft Articles on Responsibility of States for Internationally Wrongful Acts (ARSIWA), which notes that third states have a duty to 'cooperate to bring [the grave illegality] to an end through lawful means', and not to 'recognize as lawful a situation created' by the grave illegality.[94] The purpose of third-state responsibility is to prompt adherence to international law by peacefully using collective leverage against the perpetrating state.

The section outlining third-state responsibility is arguably one of the most significant paragraphs of the July 2024 ruling.[95] Building on customary international legal principles outlined in ARSIWA, the Court ruled that third-party states have 'an obligation not to recognize any changes in the physical character or demographic composition, institutional structure or status of the territory occupied by Israel on 5 June 1967…'[96] These territories include the West Bank, the Gaza Strip and East Jerusalem.

Dr Ralph Wilde, a professor specialising in public international law, summarised the implications of the ICJ ruling succinctly: 'all states, including the UK, bear special legal obligations to suppress these violations [and] to take all positive steps within their power to bring Israel's illegal presence in the OPT to an end'.

Genocide proper

How should we understand the ICJ's ruling about the illegal occupation of the OPT in the context of the ongoing genocide?

On one hand, as Francesca Albanese told the Tribunal, the UK has an obligation to stop any cooperation that may directly or indirectly assist Israel in maintaining the illegal occupation, *regardless* of the genocide in Gaza. However, that doesn't mean the ICJ's ruling in July 2024 has no relevance or bearing to the genocide in Gaza. Far from it. In light of the ruling, the UK's obligations regarding the prevention of genocide are significantly heightened precisely because 'Israel's economy of occupation has turned into an economy of genocide.'[97] When we talk about the risk of genocide, Albanese stressed, we are talking about 'Israel's entire use of force in the Gaza Strip and occupied Palestinian territory broadly'. As a result, any state that continues to engage with Israel's illegal occupation *is in turn also* failing in its duty to prevent genocide.

Vice versa, the genocide in Gaza heightens the UK's obligations relating to the non-assistance of illegal occupation. That's because the duty of non-recognition contains within it a diplomatic dimension – and it is breached by acts implying acceptance of the unlawful situation, such as treating Israel as entitled to exercise 'self-defence' in territory it occupies or annexes, or lending political cover that shields its ongoing violations from accountability.

There is a much wider point here: it is very difficult to somehow tease out specific forms of support for Israel that would be immune from obligations emanating from the ICJ.

You will often hear ministers say that their support for Israel should not be taken as support for the illegal occupation. Yet, as Ralph Wilde explained, states have an obligation not to assist an illegal presence *regardless* of the intentions of this assistance. 'Whether or not the intent behind this aid or assistance is to support illegality is irrelevant,' he stressed.

Informing Wilde's claim is something central about Israel's economic, military and political reality: the inextricable economic, military and social links between the Israeli presence in the OPT, on the one hand, and so-called Israel proper (the pre-1967 borders), on the other. In other words, it is impossible to identify discrete matters that are not linked to the Israeli presence in the OPT. Consequently, Wilde explained, the UK is obliged to 'address Israel as a general matter' and should stop providing any support to Israel whatsoever, not just support that might end up being used to commit serious violations of international law in the OPT, since any support to Israel 'is going to end up, one way or another, supporting the existence of [its illegal] occupation'.

This was echoed by Francesca Albanese, who challenged the perceived distinction between 'Israel' and 'the Occupied Palestinian Territory'. As the ICJ recognised, Israel's intention is to acquire sovereignty over the occupied Palestinian territory and to integrate the area, including the settlements, within its territory. Given that Israel has an entire infrastructure and economy that is designed to displace and replace the Palestinian people, Albanese concluded, the economic distinction between 'Israel' and 'the occupied Palestinian territory' is not meaningful. In a similar vein, then, the distinction between different kinds of support with which states provide Israel is a fiction. Support for Israel *is* support for the illegal occupation. Support for Israel *is* support for ethnic cleansing. Support for Israel *is* support for genocide.

At the heart of the ICJ's dual rulings are two fundamental obligations that are placed upon all states, including the UK. One, to prevent and to punish genocide. Two, to cooperate to bring the illegal occupation to an end. But what does this mean in practice?

Fulfilling its obligations

The UK's legal obligations require more than expressions of concern. They require, in the words of Ó Cuinn, 'the undertaking of a root and branch audit of the UK's relationship with Israel across multiple fronts, diplomatic, military, and economic, to identify where there was potential complicity or leverage that could be addressed to prevent genocide'.

Below, we list five tangible duties placed upon the UK. This list is not exhaustive. Instead, it outlines the most immediate areas in which UK government policy risks unlawful assistance, complicity or individual criminal liability.

First, the UK is obliged to immediately suspend arms transfers and related military exports where there is a serious risk of use in genocide, crimes against humanity or grave IHL violations.

The UK's export of arms, components and dual-use technology to Israel engages overlapping duties under the Arms Trade Treaty (ATT), customary IHL, the Genocide Convention, and the general law of state responsibility. Under Article 6 of the ATT, a transfer is prohibited where a state has knowledge that the items would be used in genocide, crimes against humanity or war crimes; and under Article 7, an export must be refused where, after assessment, there is an overriding risk that it would contribute to serious violations of IHL or international human rights law.[98] In April 2024, the Human Rights Council adopted a resolution in which it called upon states to 'cease the sale, transfer and diversion of arms, munitions and other military equipment to Israel'.[99]

Following the ICJ's provisional measures in January 2024 recognising a plausible risk of genocide in Gaza, the legal and factual threshold for the UK to justify continued licensing becomes exceptionally difficult to sustain.

Britain is further compelled to implement an arms embargo on the basis of the ICJ's July ruling on the illegal occupation.

In light of this ruling, the UK has the duty to impose restrictions on the trade and financing of arms, dual-use items, technology, energy, among other commodities and services, which facilitate the prolongation and entrenchment of grave illegalities committed by the state of Israel in the OPT and act as means of militarised or economic predation.

The obligation to end arms sales, then, comes from *both* the duty to prevent genocide *and* the duty not to assist in an illegal occupation. Ultimately, the totality of Israel's economy of occupation means that, in the words of Francesca Albanese, 'nothing short of a full arms embargo in Israel will suffice for the UK to start meeting its legal obligation'.

Second, the UK is obliged to suspend intelligence-sharing, training and other security cooperation that could materially assist unlawful acts. Security cooperation – including intelligence-sharing, training, joint research and operational support – may amount to unlawful assistance if it materially contributes to grave breaches, or to maintaining an unlawful occupation and apartheid regime. Under ARSIWA Article 16, responsibility can arise where a state knowingly facilitates another state's internationally wrongful acts. The Genocide Convention's prevention duty and Common Article 1 of the four Geneva Conventions further require the UK to withhold support where there is a serious risk it will contribute to prohibited conduct.

At the domestic level, the UK's Overseas Security and Justice Assistance (OSJA) guidance requires prior human-rights risk assessments and directs that assistance should be withheld where there is a clear risk that UK support might contribute to violations.[100] In the present context – where international courts and UN mechanisms have repeatedly documented patterns of serious violations – continued cooperation creates acute legal risk.

The third set of duties relate to the UK's obligation to ensure non-recognition and non-assistance in respect of Israel's unlawful presence in the OPT.

The Court ruled that all states must 'abstain from entering into economic or trade dealings with Israel concerning the occupied Palestinian territory or parts thereof' and 'to take steps to prevent trade or investment relations that assist in the maintenance of the illegal situation created by Israel'. This encompasses a comprehensive obligation on the part of third states to 'prevent trade or investment relations that assist in the maintenance of the illegal situation created by Israel in the OPT'.

This includes a review of trade and investment ties including the review of its existing trade and investment relations with Israel and Israeli entities. This does not only include trade and investment relations with the OPT but also with Israel as a whole, to the extent that these assist in the maintenance of the illegal situation. Since Israel's economy and the settlement-occupation enterprise are structurally integrated, narrow measures focused only on settlement goods are insufficient to discharge the duty of non-assistance.[101] The UK therefore has obligations to review trade and investment ties and to regulate corporate actors – including arms firms, technology companies, banks, pension funds and universities – where their conduct contributes to or benefits from maintaining unlawful occupation, apartheid, or serious IHL violations.[102] As Albanese stated in her testimony, the ICJ ruling creates a duty on states like the UK 'to cease all trade, all investment, all economic relations with the state of Israel'.

The duty of non-recognition is breached not only by formal recognition of sovereignty claims, but also by acts implying acceptance of the unlawful situation – such as treating Israel as entitled to exercise sovereign 'self-defence' powers in territory it occupies or annexes or lending political cover that shields ongoing violations from accountability. The ICJ's reasoning in the Chagos, Namibia and Wall advisory opinions – now extended to Israel's presence in the OPT as a whole – makes clear that third states must not render aid or assistance in maintaining the unlawful situation.[103] In the 2007 *Bosnia and Herzegovina* v *Serbia and Montenegro* judgement, the Court specified that states have the responsibility 'to employ all means reasonably available to them, so as to prevent genocide so far as possible', particularly those states with 'the capacity to influence effectively the action of persons likely to commit, or already committing, genocide'.[104]

Fourth, the UK must support humanitarian relief and vocally oppose policies producing famine conditions.

IHL prohibits starvation of civilians as a method of warfare and requires parties to allow and facilitate rapid and unimpeded passage of humanitarian relief for civilians. Where a state has influence, Common Article 1 requires it to act to ensure respect for these rules.[105] This generates both negative and positive obligations to ensure that the population is not deprived of objects necessary for its survival. Israel as the occupying power is not only prohibited from obstructing aid, but it is also obliged to ensure the population's needs are met, as laid out in the ICJ's Advisory Opinion in October 2025.[106]

In circumstances where credible evidence indicates a serious risk that conditions of life are being inflicted that could exacerbate humanitarian collapse – such as suspending or withholding of lifesaving assistance without adequate replacement – and potentially meet the threshold of Article II(c) of the Genocide Convention which prohibits 'deliberately inflicting on the group conditions of life calculated to bring about its physical destruction in whole or in part', the UK is legally required to introduce policies and implement practices that prevent such a situation.[107]

Fifth, the UK must cooperate fully with international mechanisms of accountability, including the ICC and ICJ, and must investigate and potentially prosecute British citizens who either participated in or were complicit with the genocide.

Francesca Albanese and Tayab Ali both drew attention to Articles 86 and 89 of the Rome Statute, which obliges the UK to cooperate with the ICC, execute arrests and surrender indicted individuals found in its territory. Where the ICC issues arrest warrants relevant to crimes committed in Gaza or the OPT, the UK has a duty to cooperate, including by arresting and surrendering suspects who enter UK territory (including aerial and water territory), subject to any applicable immunities as interpreted under the Rome Statute.

The UK does not merely have a duty *not* to obstruct efforts at achieving accountability. It has a positive duty to *support* these efforts.[108] That means preserving evidence, supporting independent investigations and protecting those tasked with documenting violations.

States and individuals

International criminal law attaches responsibility not only to states, but also to individuals. The foundational principle

– articulated at Nuremberg – is that crimes under international law are committed by persons, and accountability of individuals is necessary to enforce international norms.[109]

Under the Rome Statute, individuals may incur liability for genocide, war crimes, crimes against humanity and crimes of aggression through: (i) direct perpetration; (ii) aiding, abetting or otherwise assisting, including by providing the means for the crime; and (iii) direct and public incitement to genocide. These modes of liability are relevant where officials provide material support, authorise arms transfers, supply intelligence or make public statements that could be understood as encouraging genocidal acts.[110]

In addition, civilian managers may be liable for crimes committed by subordinates where they have effective control, are on notice of crimes and fail to take necessary and reasonable measures to prevent or repress them (the doctrine of superior responsibility). This doctrine matters for decision-making structures where responsibility is often mediated through institutional hierarchies.[111] Accordingly, the relevant authorities have an obligation to investigate government officials, including ministers, who signed off on arms licensing, intelligence operations and military deployments, and particularly all such interactions after the ICJ issued provisional measures in January 2025. In addition, authorities must investigate instances in which British citizens joined the Israeli military and participated in the genocide or are living in illegal settlements in the West Bank and East Jerusalem in contravention of the July 2024 ICJ ruling. In cases where the evidence reveals illegal acts, the investigations must lead to prosecution.

We now turn to the central question: has the UK fulfilled its legal obligations? In Chapter 5, we will learn that 'no' is a profound understatement. The truth is far starker: the UK government has been complicit, and, in certain respects, actively participated in the greatest crime of our time.

5

Complicity in Genocide

The whole world and everyone back at home is relying on you... Quite a bit of what goes on here can't necessarily be talked about all of the time. We can't necessarily tell the world what you're doing.[112]

—PRIME MINISTER KEIR STARMER

This is what Prime Minister Keir Starmer told troops while visiting RAF Akrotiri, Cyprus, in December 2024. Throughout Israel's genocide in Gaza, the UK government has responded to questions about its role with evasion, obstruction and silence. That includes the use of British military bases, support from UK surveillance aircraft, and the sale and supply of weapons that have been used to commit atrocities against Palestinians in the Gaza Strip and the West Bank.

Two months before Starmer's Cyprus visit, the government announced its partial suspension of arms to Israel. Suspending around 30 arms export licences out of a total of 350, the government made one, huge, glaring omission: the continued supply of parts for Israel's F-35 jets. This included components that went to the United States to be sent on to Israel, and spare parts that went into the global stockpiles that may then go to Israel.

To this day, the government has refused to explain how the continued supply of F-35 parts is consistent with its obligation to prevent genocide. Telling MPs repeatedly that it is not for the government to decide what constitutes genocide, the government refuses to publish the legal advice it has received. Transparency and accountability are cornerstones of democracy, yet the public have been left in the dark over the ways in which government responsibilities have been discharged. The British public deserves to know the full scale of the UK's complicity in crimes against humanity.

Israel has not been acting alone, and it is unlikely that it could have generated so much harm had Britain and its allies taken meaningful action to compel it to stop. Israel has not just relied on their silence, but also on their active military, economic and diplomatic support. Our government won't tell the public about its complicity and participation in genocide. But we will.

Arming genocide

Britain has long supplied Israel with weapons that have been used to extinguish human life and destroy vital infrastructures in Gaza, the West Bank and beyond.

Katie Fallon, the advocacy manager at the Campaign Against the Arms Trade (CAAT), documented 633 million single individual export licences for the ten-year period from 2015 to 2024. This includes aircraft, technology, grenades, bombs, missiles and military training equipment. In addition to these single licences, CAAT has gathered evidence of another 71 'unlimited value open licences', which allows for an unlimited quantity of weapons and parts. Included in this military supply, as Tayab Ali testified, is the continued sale of British petroleum to supply Israel (likely refined into jet fuel for attacks in Gaza).

The Tribunal was primarily concerned with the supply of arms between October 2023 until the present. Under the Conservative government, this totalled £48.9 million, comprising £3.9 million related to single licences and £45 million related to the transfer of UK-made components to Israel for the F-35 programme.[113] Additionally, there were four open-value licences (which do not limit the quantity or value of exports). Under the Labour government to date, the estimated value is £148 million for single licences and £162 million related to the transfer of UK-made components to Israel for the F-35 programme. From October to December 2024 alone, the value of arms export licences granted was higher than the value of what was approved by the Conservative government for the whole period from 2020 to 2023.

As uncovered by *Declassified UK*, 14 shipments of F-35 parts were sent directly from a British RAF base in Norfolk to Nevatim Air Base in Israel from October 2023 to September 2024. At least two of those shipments took place under the Labour government.

Still arming genocide

In September 2024, the Labour Foreign Secretary announced a partial suspension of arms exports to Israel. This partial suspension came with a crucial exemption: the supply of components for the global F-35 programme, to which Israel has access.

F-35 jets have played a pivotal role in Israel's genocidal assault on Gaza. Indeed, as CAAT's Fallon pointed out, on the same day that the Foreign Secretary announced that the F-35 parts would be exempted, a Danish NGO, Danwatch, revealed that an F-35 was used in July 2024 to drop three 2,000-pound bombs in an attack on a so-called 'safe zone' in Khan Younis, killing 90 men, women and children.[114]

Fallon noted that, at the time, Israel had 45 F-35s, with a further 30 on order along with F-15s and F-16s. Approximately 15 per cent of every F-35 aircraft that is produced and sold to Israel is made in the UK. At least 75 British companies are involved. Fallon outlined the reality: a huge portion of these parts are going to Israeli F-35s because of the number of sorties into Gaza and the extended flying hours that this entails; no other international partner, she maintained, is using F-35s at the same rate. Indeed, CAAT submitted a freedom of information request which revealed that the use of the Open General Export Licence for F-35 spare parts to Israel nearly tripled in 2023. Since then, Israel has used F-35s at more than five times the normal rate of peacetime operations, which explains the large quantity of spare parts that Britain provided to Israel since autumn 2023.

The UK has made an enormous contribution to the F-35 programme – and the F-35 programme has been absolutely central to Israel's genocide. Keep this in mind when the Foreign Secretary insists that the UK sends just 1 per cent of Israel's military equipment, in an attempt to downplay Britain's role in crimes against humanity. Fallon testified that the 1 per cent is 'a critical part of the jets that are being used to drop bombs'. As such, '1 per cent doesn't even begin to cover the percentage of impact that these parts have'.

Katie Fallon exposed the hypocrisy in the government's own assessment. In announcing the partial suspension, the government acknowledged that it must not grant a licence if it determines that there is a clear risk that items might be used to commit or facilitate a serious violation of IHL. Despite this assessment, the government departed from its own domestic rules in order to create its legal carve-out for the continuation of F-35 parts, which comprised over 90 per cent of the arms trade at the time. By describing the continuation of the F-35 programme as a 'carve-out', they are describing – or admitting – an exemption to their own criteria. That is, then Foreign Secretary David Lammy accepted the fact that there was a clear risk that F-35 jets might be used in violation of IHL, but that his government was not prepared to halt the supply of F-35 parts that were likely to end up in Israel. Describing this as 'unprecedented', Fallon said 'nothing like this has ever happened before where there's an admission that the legal threshold has been reached and then a complete departure from it'.

The UK government offered several – often inconsistent – explanations for why the exemption of F-35 parts was necessary. Principally, it argued that the carve-out was necessary because removing the British government from the F-35 programme would undermine international peace and security. In several statements, the government cited a 'supply-chain' issue as justification. The government repeatedly claimed that it could not withdraw from the F-35 programme, because such a suspension would undermine 'the global F-35 supply chain that is vital for the security of the UK, our allies, and NATO'.

As part of this justification, the government claimed that it was not possible to trace the destination of F-35 parts nor, therefore, prevent them from ending up in Israel. Fallon raised considerable doubt over this claim. As she explained, parts must be tracked in the event they are found to be faulty, so the claim that these parts cannot be tracked is not credible. The real reason for the exemption of F-35 parts is the lack of political will to confront the United States over the fulfilment of actionable legal obligations, namely, the obligation to prevent these parts from ending up in Israel.

On top of this, there are several compelling reasons to doubt the veracity of the government's so-called suspension itself. Rami Khayal, of the Palestinian Youth Movement, presented evidence from a report that was published in partnership with Workers for a Free Palestine and Progressive International.[115] According to the report, the UK continued to send Israel thousands of military items despite the export ban.

Using data from the Israeli Tax Authority (ITA), the report documented British arms exports to Israel covering a period from October 2023 to March 2025. The data shows that Britain had sent 8,630 separate munitions consignments since the ostensible suspension of arms trade took effect. The munitions fall under a category of import labelled 'bombs, grenades, torpedoes, mines, missiles and similar munitions of war and parts thereof'.[116] In addition to weapons and ammunition, evidence shows 6 shipments from the UK to Israel of 299 items, which the Israeli Tax Authority identifies as tanks and other armoured fighting vehicles. Khayal told the Tribunal that this contradicted David Lammy's statement in Parliament that 'much of what we send [to Israel] is defensive in nature. It is not what we describe routinely as arms'.

Relating to F-35s, the government insisted that no F-35 parts were being exported to Israel directly. However, Khayal pointed out the following peculiarity. If this were true, and given that the majority of military export licences issued over at least the past five years have been aircraft parts, then we would have expected an observable decrease in shipments following the licence suspension in September 2024. However, the report found an increase in the number of shipments following the suspension, putting the reality of the suspension into serious doubt. The report was also able to identify the established pattern of the use of courier shipments for small shipments of F-35 spare parts. The data indicates that the pattern of these monthly shipments remained steady, despite the government's claim that it had stopped the direct export of F-35 parts to Israel. While the report could not confirm that these shipments contained F-35 parts, these patterns are suggestive and demand clarification. Khayal demanded a full investigation of these shipments and called on the British government to release transparent and complete licensing and export data to clarify the nature of these goods.

John McEvoy from *Declassified UK* concluded that it was highly unlikely that the ban on direct exports of F-35 parts to Israel made a significant impact on the supply chain of F-35 parts from Britain to Israel. This was for three reasons.

One, shipping documents obtained by *Declassified UK* indicated that around 90 per cent of all F-35 exports from Britain are sent directly to the USA, where they can be exported onward to Israel.

Two, the UK is not just involved in the *supply* but also the *transfer* of arms. Even after the September arms restrictions, reports indicate that F-35 parts bound for Israel were allowed to be shipped through London Stansted airport.[117] Questions submitted to the Foreign Office about how this was allowed to happen remain unanswered.

Three, the UK has been involved in the supply of 'ammunition containers'. McEvoy revealed that an engineering firm in County Durham, Permoid, sent over 1,000 ammunition containers to Israel since October 2023. Around 300 of those containers were exported in April 2025, more than half a year after arms trade had ostensibly been suspended. Most of these containers were sent to an Elbit systems factory near Tel Aviv, which produces mortar shells for the Israeli military. As McEvoy stated, 'the UK government would seemingly have us believe that facilitating the supply of ammunition containers… is a morally justifiable and legally tenable position'.

Overflying genocide

Throughout Israel's genocide in Gaza, the UK government has remained tight-lipped about the role of British military bases. Investigative journalist Matt Kennard described RAF Akrotiri as 'the central international site for supporting and supplying Israel's genocide in Gaza'.

The RAF has conducted regular surveillance flights over Gaza and has passed this intelligence to Israel. Their take-offs and landings are not registered on any commercial flight-tracking websites but can be tracked through transponder data. Kennard noted that there had been over 600 surveillance flights by the RAF from December 2023 to September 2025.

Kennard explained how RAF flights would typically turn their transponders off as they were flying over the sea so that 'activity over Gaza stayed secret'.[118] However, on 28 July 2025, a privately contracted flight had mistakenly forgotten to turn off the transponder, enabling Kennard to see that these flights would circle an area of interest for three to four hours, in this particular case in Khan Yunis, an area that at the time was subjected to intense military activity. Israeli airstrikes were reported in the same area the following day. This example raises a crucial, wider question that has remained unanswered: has intelligence collected by the UK been used to provide information or support airstrikes that have breached international law?

We do not know exactly what British intelligence has been used for, which has generated grave concern that Britain could be complicit in actions that constitute grave breaches of international law. What we do know is that the Israeli military has cited hostage rescue as an excuse for the indiscriminate mass slaughter of Palestinians and a range of other egregious violations of IHL. In the UK's case, hostage rescue has been used as a justification to provide Israel with military assistance in the genocide. Under the Geneva Conventions and the Arms Trade Treaty – both of which Britain has signed – there is a legal obligation to ensure that any military support does not contribute to violations of IHL.

Crucially, the UK is not in control of how its intelligence is used once it is sent to Israel. 'If you're sending this information to the Israeli military in real time,' Kennard says, 'how can you then say, "Well, we only want you to use it for hostage rescue"? Once it's in Israel's hands, they can use it for whatever they want.' An anonymous Israeli official added that Britain had 'been able to provide intelligence from the air and cyberspace that Israel cannot collect on its own'.[119]

Matt Kennard's evidence was backed up by Professor

Nicos Trimikliniotis from the University of Nicosia in Cyprus. Trimikliniotis describes these RAF bases as 'infrastructures to conduct activities which may aid Israeli war crimes'. One of the most significant implications of these surveillance flights is that the UK government is in possession of information relevant to its assessment of war crimes. As Kennard told the Tribunal: '[The RAF has] one of the greatest databases of genocide in recent history.' Despite this, the government refuses to use this footage in its assessment of IHL violations.

One such violation was the killing of World Central Kitchen aid workers. The Tribunal heard from Forz Khan, the lawyer representing the parents of James Henderson, a British aid worker killed by Israeli soldiers. Khan outlined that the 'murder' is very likely to have been recorded by one of these surveillance flights and therefore had asked for the footage, but the government has refused to share it with him or the family. 'We've been told there was a flight,' Khan testified, 'but [the UK government] refused to answer anything further.' Khan is confident that the footage exists. 'The fact that you say there is something, but we can't show you,' Khan explained, 'leads us and indeed leads any reasonable person to the irresistible inference that there is something to be seen there.'

Summarising evidence from previous witnesses, Khan had no doubt that 'Britain had countenanced Israel's actions in many, many ways and that includes when there's been murder of British citizens in occupied Palestinian territories.'

The performance of surveillance flights was not the only function of RAF bases. These bases were home to huge military transport vehicles, capable of carrying tanks, helicopters, and all sorts of weaponry and personnel. 'To this day,' Kennard said, 'we do not know what was on those planes.' Kennard said that it was highly likely that military cargo has been airlifted from RAF Akrotiri to Israel. That cargo has often travelled to Cyprus from US military bases in other parts of Europe.

Kennard revealed that Israeli Air Force planes had been landing in Britain since October 2023. With transponder data, we can see that Israeli Air Force planes, which were refuelling fighter jets over Gaza, were landing in RAF Brize Norton in Oxfordshire on the way to the United States and back again.

On 27 October 2023, it was reported that the SAS, highly secretive special forces, had been deployed to Cyprus.[120] The next day, the UK military and intelligence services sent out a D-Notice, a censorship order to the media. Since that day, Kennard informed the Tribunal, we have had no information about what UK special forces have been doing in Cyprus and potentially in Gaza.

Surveillance is not the only way in which the UK has been sharing knowledge with Israel. In February 2024, the Conservative government admitted that there were 'currently six Israeli Armed Forces officers posted in the UK', adding that: 'Israel is represented by Armed Forces personnel in its Embassy in the UK, and as participants in UK defence-led training courses.'[121] When asked about the ranks of these personnel, the Defence Minister stated that 'this information is being withheld in order to protect personal information and to avoid prejudicing relations between the United Kingdom and another State'.

In June 2025, the Parliamentary Under-Secretary of State for Defence, Luke Pollard MP, confirmed in a reply to a written parliamentary question that 'as part of routine Defence engagement with Israel, the UK is currently training a limited number of Israel Defense Forces personnel on UK-based training courses'.[122]

McEvoy revealed to the Tribunal that Israeli military officers have been allowed to train in Britain at the prestigious Royal College of Defence Studies (RCDS) since 2023. Moreover, he explained that the government chose to exempt components for trainer aircraft from its licence suspensions. They were exempted on the grounds that they were not for use in the current conflict in Gaza. However, Israeli pilots rely on UK-made parts to learn to fly the fighter jets, which were used in the destruction and genocide of Gaza. Shipping documents have revealed how an aerospace firm in Wolverhampton has sent at least ten shipments of M346 Lavy components used for training to Israel since December 2024. The M346 Lavy is a high-performance aircraft designed to train pilots to fly advanced fighter jets, including the F-16 and the F-35.

In addition to training, the UK government has also welcomed several high-ranking Israeli officers to Britain since October 2023, presumably to discuss arms transfer, Israel's use of UK military bases in Cyprus and Britain, surveillance support and intelligence-sharing. The government has provided these officers with special diplomatic immunity to protect them from private arrest applications under universal jurisdiction legislation. That list includes Lieutenant General Herzi Halevi (the IDF's then Chief of the General Staff, who had been directing the Israeli military's operations throughout the Gaza genocide), Major General Oded Bassiuk (head of the Israeli military's operations directorate), and Major General Tomer Bar (the commander of the Israeli Air Force). These visits were intended to occur in secrecy, and there are presumably other Israeli military officers who have visited the UK.

Funding genocide

This system of oppression could not [have been] and has not been sustained without the complicit active support of Western governments, public bodies, companies and corporations.

—BEN JAMAL

Israel would not have been able to carry out its genocide against the Palestinian people without continued economic support from countries and corporations around the world. The Tribunal heard from Richard Burgon MP, who has consistently called for the UK government to ban all trade in goods and services with illegal Israeli settlements and impose targeted sanctions, including travel bans and asset freezes on all individuals and entities complicit in Israel's occupation, in adherence with international law. 'The government should have been using every single tool at its disposal, from sanctions to using its role in the UN and elsewhere, to force – not plead – with Israel to stop,' Burgon said.

Regarding sanctions, Burgon drew particular attention to the UK's double standards towards Russia, where the government has sanctioned over 2,500 individuals, entities and ships under the Russia sanctions regime, over 2,300 of which have been sanctioned since Putin's full-scale invasion. By contrast, with respect to Israel, the government has ordered sanctions against two far-right ministers and a handful of extreme settlers and settler bodies. It is worth noting that these actions were taken largely in response to Israeli activity in the West Bank, rather than Gaza. Burgon concluded that the government's failure to take action against Israel's use of force in Gaza was proof of economic and political complicity.

This was echoed by Sara Husseini, who said that 'without any kind of economic or diplomatic sanctions, Israel will never be compelled to abide by its international obligations as set out in the ICJ Advisory Opinion on the legal consequences of Israel's prolonged occupation'. Husseini highlighted the government's eventual announcement of the suspension of trade negotiations with Israel in May 2025, underscoring that this suspension was 'limited and temporary'. The government's approach was made apparent by the fact that, just a week later, it sent a trade envoy to Israel, who announced on social media that he was in Israel to 'promote trade with the UK'.[123]

While economic support to Israel has flowed over the past two and a half years, Britain has failed to sufficiently support the flow of humanitarian aid to starving Palestinians. Husseini condemned the Conservative government's appalling decision to suspend support for UNRWA at a time when Palestinians needed their services the most. She noted that some funding was restored by the Labour government, although at lower than previous levels, despite the greatly increased need. Moreover, the British government failed to defend UNRWA from attacks and smear campaigns led by the Israeli government.

Justifying genocide

I think Israel does have that right.
—PRIME MINISTER KEIR STARMER

Speaking in October 2023, Keir Starmer told LBC's Nick Ferrari that Israel had the right to cut off water and electricity to the besieged population of Gaza.[124] While a particularly egregious example, this is no anomaly of British foreign policy. In response to the clearly articulated intention to commit acts of grave violation of international law, Britain has been 'concerned' about Israel's security and maintained a position of 'unequivocally backing Israel's right to defend itself'.[125] The Foreign Secretary has reiterated the government's support for Israel's 'right to defend itself', yet has consistently failed to offer sufficient specificity about what this means, let alone how it should be exercised within the boundaries of international law. We note that, when it comes to Palestinians, similar phrases are missing from the British government's lexicon.

Sara Husseini, Director of the British Palestinian Committee, cites the persistent invocation by the British government of 'the self-defence rhetoric invoked by an occupying power against an occupied people'. We should not underestimate the significance of this support, which helped Israel accrue both the confidence and the political capital it needed to execute its operations with impunity. Equipped with the backing of Western governments, Israel was able routinely to deploy the language of self-defence to justify its crimes.

Starmer's infamous endorsement of Israel's right to cut off food and water to the entire population of Gaza is part of a much wider package of political support that both the Conservative and Labour governments have given to Israel. Long before the start of the genocide, Britain has provided Israel with not only the military means for carrying out its atrocities, but also with the political and diplomatic support it has relied on to act with impunity. This support is summarised neatly by Husseini. 'Ongoing diplomatic support for Israel,' she says, has entailed 'justifications for atrocities being committed, dehumanisation of Palestinians in political rhetoric, efforts to undermine Palestinian attempts at accountability [and] the demonisation of international solidarity.'

Exonerating genocide

On 20 May 2024, ICC Chief Prosecutor Karim Khan announced his intention to file applications for arrest warrants against Hamas leaders Yahya Sinwar, Mohammed Deif and Ismail Haniyeh and Israeli leaders Prime Minister Benjamin Netanyahu and Minister of Defence Yoav Gallant. On 21 November, the ICC issued arrest warrants for Benjamin Netanyahu, Yoav Gallant and Mohammed Deif (by that time Israel had killed Sinwar and Haniyeh). 'With regard to the crimes, the [Court's Pre-Trial Chamber] found reasonable grounds to believe that Mr. Netanyahu... and Mr. Gallant... bear criminal responsibility for the following crimes as co-perpetrators for committing the acts jointly with others: the war crime of starvation as a method of warfare; and the crimes against humanity of murder, persecution, and other inhumane acts.'

Tayab Ali, the Director of ICJP, claimed in his testimony that Britain had not just failed in its obligations to support the ICC, but actively 'undermined' the court by questioning its jurisdiction, withholding support for arrest warrants and failing to facilitate investigations. This applies to both Conservative and Labour governments. In June 2024, the Conservative government challenged the ICC's jurisdiction over Israeli nationals. The challenge was unsuccessful, but it resulted in the delay of arrest warrants. Ali also drew attention to a report by *Middle East Eye* showing that David Cameron, while he was Foreign Secretary under the Conservative government, 'directly threatened the prosecutor in relation to the Palestine investigation', which, if proven, 'would amount to direct state interference in judicial independence, a flagrant breach of Britain's obligations under the Rome Statute'.

Ali criticised the UK Labour government for failing to show any 'formal or unofficial' support for the ICC prosecutor, Karim Khan, who is a British citizen, as he was coming under unprecedented attack and sanctions by the United States. 'By failing to defend the prosecutor, condemn sanctions, or shield the court from interference,' Ali said, 'Britain has not only betrayed the victims of Gaza, but actively undermined the very institution designed to deliver justice.'

Former Ecuadorian Foreign Minister Guillaume Long outlined the ways in which the UK had 'chosen political convenience over legal obligations'. He highlighted the requirements of the ICC arrest warrants and the prevention of genocide. Principally, he drew attention to the UK's refusal to exercise its universal jurisdiction powers to initiate a domestic investigation or prosecution into war crimes in Gaza. This complements Kennard's evidence regarding a lack of transparency about whether intelligence collected by British surveillance aircraft has been shared with Israel but not the ICC.

Sara Husseini of the British Palestinian Committee explained how government ministers have consistently refused to support the South African submission at the ICJ in its case against Israel, and how the government did not change its policies after the January 2024 court ruling that it was plausible that Israel was committing genocide. From its refusal to stand up for the ICC, to its effective denial of the ICJ rulings, the British government has failed to support those institutions attempting to hold the perpetrators accountable for genocide and has consequently undermined the legal norms obliging warring parties to protect civilians and civilian sites.

Normalising genocidal apartheid

The Tribunal heard from Richard Falk, who previously served as United Nations Special Rapporteur on the situation of human rights in the Palestinian territories occupied since 1967, and is currently the chair of the board of trustees at the Euro-Mediterranean Human Rights Monitor. Falk spoke on behalf of the 'Gaza People's Tribunal', which was holding its final session the following month at Istanbul University. Falk drew a distinction between diplomatic support and 'diplomatic complicity'. He said that examples of diplomatic complicity were acts of 'treating Israel as a normal state', 'the failure to condemn Israel for what it has been doing', and the failure to 'take concrete steps in light of that condemnation'. Falk told the Tribunal that Israel should be (and should have been) suspended from the United Nations: 'As long as Israel can have the legitimacy of a sovereign member of the UN without being suspended for its non-compliance with UN directives, there is no effective means to curtail its policies.'

The genocide should have been the end of Britain's diplomatic relations with Israel. Instead, by maintaining military, diplomatic and economic support for Israel, Britain not only normalised genocide, but the apartheid state that was carrying it out. Sara Husseini drew attention to the UK's response to the ICJ July 2024 ruling that Israel's occupation of Gaza and the West Bank was illegal. Husseini stressed that the UK has yet to formally admit that Israel's laws, policies and practices meet the legal definition of apartheid, let alone 'take the appropriate and effective action to remedy this crime'. In September 2024, Britain abstained on the UN General Assembly's vote to adopt the ICJ's findings. Even before the ICJ ruling was made, the United Kingdom asked the court to reject the request for any such Advisory Opinion to be made, submitting a written statement on 20 July 2023, that read: 'The United Kingdom invites the Court to exercise its discretion and decline to respond to the Request.'[126]

Contrast Britain's willingness to support an illegal occupier to its shameful approach to Palestinian self-determination. Husseini drew attention to the prime minister's statement on 29 July 2025, regarding the conditional recognition of the state of Palestine in September, *unless* Israel agreed to a ceasefire in Gaza, resumed humanitarian aid and refrained from further annexations in the West Bank. According to Husseini, this 'symbolic and conditional recognition' was not just insufficient in the context of an ongoing genocide, it also did nothing to safeguard the Palestinian people's inalienable right to self-determination and actively undermined international law 'by casting the right to self-determination and the illegality of the occupation as negotiable'. The prime minister's statement was typical of the government's 'performative and cynical attempt to diffuse the pressure [it had] been facing in its role in Gaza' and to frame Palestinian basic rights as if they were a privilege that could be given or taken at the whim of those in power.

Silencing anti-genocide

The British government has attempted to systematically silence British citizens protesting for peace; Sara Husseini underscored the scale and significance of draconian government policies, particularly during Labour's tenure, that severely restricted peaceful protests and expressions of solidarity. The result, as she summarised, is that 'demonstrators now potentially face years in prison for protesting this country's involvement in the mass murder of women, men and children'. Husseini also claimed that the government has 'remained silent' as students and employees have faced disciplinary action and even policy intervention for participating in peaceful demonstrations for Palestine. In August 2024, it was reported that Israeli embassy officials attempted to pressure the Attorney-General's office to intervene in UK court cases relating to the prosecution of protestors. There are two particularly notorious examples of the criminalisation of pro-Palestinian protest.

In January 2025, the Palestine Solidarity Campaign (PSC) organised a demonstration in Whitehall. Ahead of the demonstration, the police banned the planned march to the BBC. On the day, demonstrators were confronted with extremely heavy-handed and aggressive policing. At the end of the rally, it was announced from the stage that a delegation of organisers and rally speakers – including an 87-year-old Jewish Holocaust survivor – would walk silently and peacefully towards the BBC. PSC have publicly attested to what happened next:

> When the delegation reached the police line [at the end of Whitehall], they were not stopped as expected but were instead invited to proceed into Trafalgar Square by the police who said, 'please filter through'. When the delegation

reached the other end of the square, they encountered a line of police which prevented them from going any further. They formally requested that the delegation – a maximum of 25 people – be allowed to proceed. The police officer in charge said he would need to 'pass this up the line for a decision'. While the delegation was awaiting that response, the police violently and for no apparent reason arrested the chief steward of the rally, Chris Nineham. At this point, the delegation laid their flowers as they had said they would do and dispersed, and Ben Jamal and Ismail Patel used a megaphone to call on the crowd that had gathered around them to do the same, which people then did. At no stage was there any organised breach of the conditions imposed by the police. There is a large amount of video evidence confirming all of these events.

A total of 77 people were arrested on the day, 66 of them for alleged violations of police orders. Among them were Chris Nineham (the vice-chair of the Stop the War Coalition). He was charged with breaching conditions, alongside Palestine Solidarity Campaign director Ben Jamal and others. In April 2026, Chris Nineham and Ben Jamal were found guilty of all charges against them. This seems an apt place, then, to share a section of Ben Jamal's testimony from the Tribunal:

> The last two years have demonstrated another truth asserted for decades by Palestinian civil society that their struggle for liberation is integral to all struggles against systems of oppression. Eric Cantona, one of my personal heroes, spoke to this truth recently when he said, 'If Gaza is lost, then humanity is lost.' If this genocide is allowed to unfold to its last stages, or even if stopped, if Israel's system

> of racist domination continues to be supported, then the wider struggles against the far rights and their doctrines of ethno-nationalism, the battle for the preservation of any system of international law, and the battle to preserve fundamental democratic freedoms, including the right to protest, will also be irreparably damaged if not lost forever.

In July 2025, it became illegal to support the civil disobedience group, Palestine Action, after being proscribed as a terrorist organisation. In doing so, the government ignored UN experts who urged the 'United Kingdom not to misuse terrorism laws against protest group Palestine Action'.[127] Following the proscription, more than 2,500 people have been arrested in connection with protests linked to Palestine Action. The vast majority have been arrested for holding placards with the words: 'I oppose genocide, I support Palestine Action.' This includes vicars, doctors and teachers. The youngest person to be arrested is 18. The eldest is 87.

In November 2025, two months after the Tribunal, eight people – who had been incarcerated for alleged pro-Palestine protest action – began a hunger strike. They were being held on remand for alleged direct action at Elbit Systems UK's Filton research or RAF Brize Norton. A month later, more than 50 MPs and Peers joined Jeremy Corbyn in writing to the Foreign Secretary to immediately meet with the lawyers of those on hunger strike, in light of growing concerns over their deteriorating health. The government refused, stating that 'it would not be appropriate' to meet while the prisoners are subject to ongoing legal proceedings. The last hunger striker ended their action in January 2026. In February, the High Court ruled that the government's proscription of Palestine Action was 'disproportionate and unlawful'.[128] The following month, at least 500 more people were arrested during a demonstration against the ban.

This is not the only example of the British government witnessing actions of solidarity – and choosing to stand on the other side. Another example is the government's failure to support citizen-led attempts to bring aid to Gaza, known as the flotilla missions. Fran Heathcote of the Public and Commercial Services Union (PCS) drew attention to the Israeli interception of the *Madleen* when the British civilian ship was en route to Gaza to provide humanitarian aid. Despite the ship being protected under international maritime law, Heathcote pointed out, this infringement 'appears to have gone unanswered by the UK government'.

Hiding genocide

For the first eleven months of the genocide, the UK government assessed that there was no clear risk that UK weapons might be used to commit or facilitate a serious violation of IHL. This assessment was used to justify why it did not have reservations about dramatically increasing weapons transfers to Israel after October 2023.

Mark Smith was a British Foreign Office official who resigned in protest over continued arms sales to Israel in August 2024. Smith was the lead official on the UK arms export licensing report, which assessed whether the UK was legally compliant. 'What I witnessed while working on that report was profoundly concerning,' Smith told the Tribunal. Smith's role was to gather all relevant information on the situation, including the airstrikes, the precision of the strikes and civilian casualties. His assessment was clear: 'it was impossible to see how the UK government was acting legally'. However, his concerns were repeatedly ignored or downplayed. Smith said that he 'could not understand how the team were justifying [the licensing], because it was very clear that Israel was in breach of IHL and even committing war crimes'. He told the Tribunal:

> While I was working on the report, I was routinely asked to change the report. This was not to correct mistakes or to ensure accuracy, as would normally be the case with a civil service report, but I was actually asked to alter the wording and placement of paragraphs and to omit key information so that it – quote unquote – sounded less bad. This is absolutely counter to what we are trained to do as civil servants, and it's something that I have never witnessed in my career.
>
> Those sections that I'd written which talked about civilian casualties, for example, I was asked to kind of play them down, make them smaller, put them towards the end of the report… I was very very, very troubled by this and I raised it at the time. … [W]e were told to delay the submission of the report until we could find something more positive to add. So this would often happen when there was a particularly appalling example of civilian deaths. There would be this… panic in the department, and we would… try to get the government in question to give us some kind of assurance that there was, let's say, an investigation going to be happening into the incident, and then we could put the investigation and all of that front and centre of the report to make it look like something good was kind of happening. So, we would delay the report until we could find something positive to put in it… Everyone wanted to make it look as though we were on the right side of the law.

> And any kind of suggestion that maybe we weren't, tended to be met with this kind of panic and a kind of extreme pressure to not talk about that.

Characterising the department's culture as one of panic and denial, Smith revealed that 'there have been hundreds if not thousands of conversations on the most controversial aspects of our arms sales policy, which will never be seen by the public'. Smith described the system as 'completely unfit for purpose', saying, 'there's no oversight. There's no independent governance. It's all left up to civil servants under immense pressure from ministers'. He also described members being asked to not voice their concerns in writing, ostensibly due to fear that information about wrongdoing would be leaked. He described how he and other colleagues made several attempts to the whistle-blowing team but were ignored. 'The only choice I had was to resign.'

Smith was not the only staff member to express concerns about UK government policy. We also heard from Fran Heathcote, general secretary of the Public and Commercial Services Union (PCS), which represents around 190,000 members working mainly within the civil service and related areas. PCS represents members who work in the Foreign Office, Home Office, Ministry of Defence, and Department of Business and Trade. The union exists to protect the interests of its members, which includes stepping in when its members are asked to perform functions that can put them at risk of violating the law.

'We don't believe,' Heathcote explained, 'that it is in the interests of our members to be placed in situations where they are potentially being asked to act in breach of the law.' PCS has raised concerns about the legality of the work being undertaken within government ministries and departments, which involves ostensibly illegal arms trade and other interactions with the government of Israel. Specifically, that includes the government's decision to continue to approve arms export licences to Israel and to continue negotiations on a free trade agreement.

On 16 May 2025, 310 staff in the Foreign, Commonwealth and Development Office (FCDO) wrote to the then Foreign Secretary, David Lammy, raising a range of concerns and calling for substantive and tangible actions to address them.[129] Those concerns included Israel's violations of IHL and potential UK government complicity with these violations. The letter called on the Foreign Secretary to urgently consider with the utmost seriousness those recommendations. Heathcote describes the response from the government as 'nothing short of a disgrace'. The government's response was to offer FCDO staff conversations with HR and counsellors with suggestions that civil servants may wish to resign if they're uncomfortable with what they're being asked to do. Heathcote describes this as 'a dereliction of duty and a startling ignorance of the provisions of the civil service code which require all civil servants to act in accordance with the law including international law'.

The testimonies of Smith and Heathcote reflect a much wider, systemic problem with the UK's legal methodology, as outlined by Charlotte Andrews-Briscoe, a lawyer at Global Legal Action Network (GLAN). 'I want to begin by saying that it's been really quite shocking to observe how far this government is willing to create legal absurdities to defy logic… to employ every tool at its disposal in order to keep arming Israel.' Andrews-Briscoe started by outlining the UK's strategic export licensing criteria: licences must be refused if there exists a risk that the item might be used to commit or facilitate a serious violation of international humanitarian law.

One of the ways the government abdicated its legal responsibilities, Andrews-Briscoe explained, was by adopting a skewed methodology for assessing violations of IHL. Instead of looking at a series of incidents and patterns of attacks, the government restricts itself to conducting an incident-by-incident assessment, focusing on trees but refusing to look at the forest. Put differently, it assessed whether a particular strike on a hospital was lawful, for example, but refused to assess the lawfulness of the decimation of the whole healthcare system.

This goes some way to explaining the bankruptcy of the government's legal methodology. By September 2024, the UK government had examined just 413 incidents of over 10,000 air strikes in Gaza, that is about 4 per cent of all attacks. Of those 413 incidents, it found only one possible violation of IHL: the World Central Kitchen attack that killed foreign aid workers, including a British citizen, in April 2024. Scores of crimes against Palestinians, however, did not qualify as breaches of IHL in the eyes of the British government. Such acts as the sniping and killing of a grandmother as she walked with her grandson holding his hand waving a white flag; the execution of Palestinians in their hospital beds by Israeli forces disguised as healthcare workers; the whole-scale flattening of bakeries apparently did not meet the threshold of violation according to this thinly veiled racist assessment.[130]

There was another, fundamental problem with the government's methodology: it based its analysis on evidence provided by Israel, the party that allegedly perpetrated the crime and has repeatedly meted justifications based on fabrications. One well-known case is the repeated bombing and invasion of Al Shifa Hospital, Gaza's largest medical centre. Israel circulated 'evidence' that Hamas's command centre was located in tunnels under the hospital, but even after it bombed the hospital and its soldiers invaded it, the military could not provide any evidence that Hamas had been misusing the hospital, let alone using it to shield its command centre. As Professor Nick Maynard attested, 'this propaganda is being repeated by our media, being repeated by our government', despite the fact that 'there is no verifiable, no remotely credible evidence to support those contentions'. As someone who has had 'unlimited access to every square inch of these hospitals', Professor Maynard told the Tribunal that it was 'inconceivable to me that they are being used as Hamas command centres'.

Notwithstanding repeated instances where the Israeli military spokesperson lied to legitimise unlawful attacks, the government decided that it could only make assessments of IHL violations based on information supplied by Israel. This was, of course, wholly unnecessary, given the extensive amount of evidence of atrocity crimes gathered by a wide array of actors, including video footage and statements of clear genocidal intent by Israeli officials. In addition, when Israel declined to supply information about specific allegations of egregious violations of international law, the government concluded that this refusal was reasonable. This set in motion what Andrews-Briscoe describes as 'circular reasoning', which saw the government repeatedly give the perpetrator of atrocities the opportunity not to incriminate themselves.

The government's use of this unscrupulous strategy was corroborated by Richard Burgon MP, who questioned several ministers about assessments of IHL violations. Burgon read the response he received from the minister responsible, Hamish Falconer MP:

> We have not been able to reach a determination in relation to the conduct of hostilities due to the lack of sufficient verifiable evidence. To determine a possible breach in this area requires access to sensitive specific information related to individual incidents such as the intended targets, anticipated military advantage and anticipated civilian harm which is often not available to us.

As Burgon rhetorically asked the Tribunal, 'Why are we asking a state whose leader and Defence Minister were charged with war crimes to provide evidence about strikes that could constitute war crimes?' Burgon points to blatant double standards regarding the UK's assessment of war crimes in Gaza compared to war crimes in Russia. He recalled how, in one parliamentary session, a government minister maintained that it is only for the courts to decide whether war crimes have taken place, and in a subsequent statement to the House, the same minister would have little trouble proclaiming that Russia has committed war crimes. Burgon characterised this as proof of 'political complicity'.

Denying genocide

In October 2023, the Palestinian human rights organisation Al-Haq and the Global Legal Action Network launched a legal case against the UK government. The case gained prominence after September 2024 when the government was forced to defend its F-35 exemption. Al-Haq's legal challenge was heard in the High Court in May 2025 but was unsuccessful.

One of the key questions in this litigation was the government's assessment of the risk of genocide. Al-Haq's case against the government's carve-out was simple: the continued transfers of F-35 parts were inconsistent with the government's duty to prevent genocide.

The government repeatedly claimed it could not determine whether there was a risk of genocide because 'the UK's long-standing policy is that any formal determination as to whether genocide has occurred is a matter for a competent national or international court rather than for governments or non-judicial bodies; it should be decided after consideration of all the evidence available in the context of a credible judicial process'. There are numerous problems with this response.

First, it need not be proven that genocide *has* taken place to trigger Britain's legal obligations. That is because Britain has a legal obligation to *prevent* genocide when there is a plausible *risk* of genocide taking place.

Across the Tribunal, there was widespread consensus that what has happened in Gaza constitutes a genocide. This consensus also includes the largest professional association in the field, the International Association of Genocide Scholars, as well as Amnesty International, Human Rights Watch and numerous UN officials. However, whether the government agrees with this growing consensus is beside the point. As the government knew full well, it did not need to wait for a court to declare that genocide had *taken* place to know that it had to act, immediately, to *prevent genocide from taking place*. As Dr Raz Segal (Associate Professor of Holocaust and Genocide Studies) explained, the Genocide Convention is activated 'not only when there's clearly genocide but when there's a clear risk of genocide'. Britain was denying that genocide had taken place, but that wasn't the point. What mattered was that the ICJ had determined that there was a clear risk of genocide taking place – and Britain was refusing to fulfil its obligations to prevent it.

At every available opportunity, ministers have been reminded of these obligations to prevent genocide. And at every opportunity, the government hid behind the same, evasive response: it is up to the courts – not them – to determine whether genocide has taken place. For Dr Gearóid Ó Cuinn, of the Global Legal Action Network (GLAN), this was how the government strove to derail attempts made by parliamentarians to ask for information on how the UK is fulfilling its duty to prevent genocide. MPs have been 'misdirected', he said, through the offer of 'a stock answer that switches the focus to how a determination of genocide is made rather than the steps that the UK government has already taken'. In doing so, Ó Cuinn stated, the government has been 'deploying a legal absurdity to sidestep requests for information on how the duty to prevent genocide is being discharged now'.

To make matters worse, government lawyers in court would then frequently direct people back to Parliament. As Ó Cuinn explained, this created a cycle 'where the court defers to Parliament and in turn the government short circuits parliamentary scrutiny'. In Parliament, the government says it's for the courts to decide whether Israel is committing genocide, and in court it says it's for the government to decide. Ó Cuinn aptly characterised this as 'a merry-go-round of delay and inaction' that gave legal cover to the government's assessment and allowed them to prevent the court from scrutinising their actions.

Ó Cuinn was clear about the government's motivations of this 'duplicity': to shield itself from having to implement its obligations to prevent genocide. The government's repeated deflections and misdirections in Parliament have happened 'so frequently and consistently', Ó Cuinn said, that 'it amounts to a purposeful tactic to avoid speaking about the fact that the UK has conducted its own assessment and to avoid having to share whether the risk of genocide has been monitored and acted upon by the government'.

Third, and perhaps most damning, the government was lying when it claimed it had not conducted its own assessment of genocide. As Ó Cuinn explained, 'government lawyers argued the very opposite' in court, admitting that they had indeed conducted their own assessment. In May 2025, UK government lawyers said that no violation of the duty to prevent a genocide 'can occur unless and until there is actually a genocide'.[131] The government *had* in fact made an assessment under the Genocide Convention, despite denying having done so in Parliament. Their conclusion? There was no serious risk of genocide.

There is another way of putting this: the British government has denied genocide. Lawyers claimed that while Israel's conduct in Gaza could 'in principle, satisfy the physical component of genocide', it was unknowable whether these 'actions are motivated by genocidal intent' and that 'no evidence has been seen that Israel is deliberately targeting civilian women or children'.[132] As Ó Cuinn summarised, the UK government had chosen to ignore blatant IHL violations, withheld critical evidence, and used an unfit methodology to assess Israel's compliance with international humanitarian law, deploying this methodology to make a determination that genocide is not occurring in Gaza.

Indeed, in a letter dated 1 September 2025, the then Foreign Secretary David Lammy stated that 'the crime of genocide occurs only where there is specific "intent to destroy, in whole or in part, a national, ethnic, racial or religious group"' and that 'the government has not concluded that Israel is acting with that intent'.[133] A year earlier, in October 2024, David Lammy replied to a Conservative MP in the House of Commons, who asked: 'Will the Foreign Secretary take this opportunity to say that there is not a genocide occurring in the Middle East?' David Lammy told Parliament that 'those terms were largely used when millions of people lost their lives in crises such as Rwanda and the Holocaust of the Second World War', adding that 'the way that people are now using those terms undermines their seriousness'. His implication was clear: not enough people had died for it to constitute a genocide. There is a term for this: genocide denial. If genocide denial is the final stage of genocide, then we are left with no doubt: the British government has been complicit and, in certain respects, participated in genocide from beginning to end.

6

A Reckoning for Genocide

Gaza has been failed by our government. I and many other healthcare workers have given detailed photographic evidence to senior members of this government and the previous government, and it has been ignored. They need to decide whether they want to believe the multiple witness testimonies from healthcare workers such as me who've got no axe to grind. We've got no political agenda. We're humanitarians. We are telling them as we see it. Or do they want to believe the Israeli propaganda which is repeatedly being regurgitated by our media... It is unconscionable that our government has not called for a full arms embargo. It is unconscionable that F-35 jets for which our government is still supplying parts are bombing those very children who I have had to operate on in Nasser Hospital and Al-Aqsa Hospital. It is unconscionable that they are still flying reconnaissance flights over Gaza, giving military intelligence to facilitate the bombing of Nasser Hospital.

—PROFESSOR NICK MAYNARD

The testimonies have uncovered a fraction of the level of suffering that Palestinians have endured. Their words will never be able to truly capture the horrors. This was no war aiming at defeating a military opponent. This was a genocide aimed at destroying a people in whole or in part – aided and abetted by the British government. The inhumanity should haunt us all forever.

Since the start of the genocide, and indeed long before, Britain has not only provided Israel with military means to carry out its atrocities but also with the political and diplomatic support Israel has relied on to act with impunity. This chapter reaches three main conclusions. First, and at the very least, the British government has catastrophically failed to fulfil its legal obligations relating to the prevention of genocide and its duty to stop all assistance to Israel's illegal occupation. More than that, the government has been complicit in genocide, apartheid and occupation. Finally, evidence suggests that the government has been an active participant in genocide.

The lasting harm of this genocide will be generational – and felt for a very long time to come. The scars of war don't disappear with the silence of the canons. We mourn for the dead – and seek justice for the living.

Complicity or participation?

The title of the tribunal is 'an inquiry into British complicity', but in light of my research, it crosses a line to participation.

—MATT KENNARD

The British government, under the Conservatives and Labour, has failed to fulfil a range of legal obligations under international law, most notably in its obligation to prevent and punish genocide. Francesca Albanese summarised: 'States including the United Kingdom have been on notice for decades of their obligations and they have not acted accordingly... They have an obligation to respect and ensure respect of international humanitarian law, and they have miserably failed this mission.' Echoing this, Tayab Ali told the Tribunal that 'every state has a legal obligation to act' and that 'Britain has failed on every single count'.

This failure is not a secret: the government has routinely admitted that it is making an exception to its legal obligations to prevent genocide, in relation to its continued participation in the F-35 programme. As Ó Cuinn explained, the duty to prevent genocide is a 'fundamental' obligation that 'should not be superseded by contractual obligations with US weapons manufacturers who are producing Israel's war plane of choice'. The government disagreed; its lawyers argued that preserving the British role in the F-35 jet fighter programme *takes precedence* over the need to comply with UK laws on arms export controls, or any UK obligation to prevent genocide. If that isn't an admission that the UK government is failing to fulfil its obligations, what is? In the words of Ó Cuinn, this is 'indicative of a government that is not compliant with the UK's legal obligations, especially the duty to prevent genocide'. Going one step further, Ralph Wilde claimed that the UK has not only failed to fulfil its legal obligations, but has *denied*, or at least refused to acknowledge, these legal obligations even exist.

Remember, the obligation is to prevent *and punish* genocide. Guillaume Long, former Foreign Minister of Ecuador, concluded that the UK has failed to fulfil this latter obligation too, given it has not initiated a single domestic investigation or prosecution into war crimes in Gaza, nor exercised its universal jurisdiction powers to pursue perpetrators of crimes in Gaza. Following the January 2024 ICJ ruling, which indicated that it was plausible that Israel was carrying out genocide, the government failed to provide clear guidelines on how it intended to meet its obligations to prevent genocide, and then failed to fulfil those obligations to prevent genocide.

The failure to punish genocide is intimately linked to the failure to prevent it. 'The longer the UK retains its ties with Israel,' Albanese said, 'the more it contributes to legitimising and normalising the illegal and the festering of impunity.' The dehumanisation of Palestinians in political rhetoric, the justification of Israel's criminal actions, the hosting of Israeli officials, the failure to support international attempts at accountability, and the criminalisation of international solidarity with the Palestinians is a very partial list of the way the British government has enabled Israel to act with total impunity.

By maintaining economic ties with Israel, Britain has also failed in its obligations to ensure non-recognition and non-assistance with respect to Israel's unlawful presence in the OPT. Britain has not just been complicit in genocide, but also in the maintenance of a system of illegal occupation, ethnic cleansing and apartheid.

To say that Britain has failed in its duties to prevent genocide and bring about an end to the illegal occupation is one way of putting it. Another is to say that because Britain continues to provide military, economic and diplomatic support to Israel, it has been *complicit* in war crimes, crimes against humanity and genocide committed by Israel.

Many of our witnesses reached this conclusion, including Tayab Ali, who in his testimony stated that: 'Britain has substantially facilitated international crimes and crossed into the territory of complicity.' Likewise, Albanese said that Britain's failure to abide by long-standing international obligations 'alone might be sufficient to establish a case for criminal complicity in the actions of Israel'.

Complicity can mean many different things – being 'involved' in war crimes can take many different forms. For some, complicity is about *assistance*. 'I was asked to give an opinion on the question of whether Britain has fulfilled its legal obligations,' Tayab Ali concluded. 'The answer is a clear no. Not only has it not fulfilled its legal obligations, the United Kingdom government has totally breached international criminal and UK criminal law, and its legal obligations under the Genocide Convention.'

Others went further. As Matt Kennard stated:

> The title of the tribunal is an inquiry into British complicity but I've been covering the military and intelligence support to Israel for nearly 2 years now during the genocide, and I used the word complicity for a while, but having looked at the evidence and studied it and investigated it, I think it definitely crosses a line to participation.

That is, the UK government has taken action to facilitate and enable war crimes, crimes against humanity and genocide.

Likewise, Ó Cuinn called the UK 'a participant' in 'Israel's atrocities against the Palestinian people', testifying that Britain had 'facilitated' genocide by 'keeping Israeli war planes supplied and UK Israeli cooperation free from scrutiny'. Rami Khayal agreed: 'Britain has played and continues to play a key role in this genocide beyond complicity. It has provided the means to carry it out.'

There is another way to describe Britain's policies relating to Gaza: anti-Palestinian racism. Complicity and participation in genocide would not be countenanced by a government that treated Palestinians as human beings worthy of protection. Evidencing a prime example of 'entrenched structural racism against Palestinians in the UK', Sara Husseini criticised the government for its refusal to set up a family visa scheme for Palestinians in Gaza, based on the Ukrainian model, despite cross-party support and more than 100,000 signatures to a parliamentary petition. This preceded the government's decision to suspend refugee family reunions altogether, the only legal route for spouses and children to join their loved ones. From its invocation of Israel's right to 'self-defence' that was used as an excuse to pummel an entire civilian population, to the support for cutting off food and water, to the condemnation of Palestinian solidarity, the British government has exposed its own failure to treat Israeli and Palestinian lives with equal worth. In many respects, judging by the government's actions and policies, the government has all but declared to the world that Palestinian lives do not matter.

What could Britain have done?

Imagine a world in which Britain took international law seriously.

Britain could have imposed a total arms embargo the moment the ICJ found a plausible risk of genocide, including halting all arms exports, dual-use items and surveillance technologies.

Britain could have ended all surveillance flights and intelligence cooperation with Israel unless intelligence was being shared with the ICC for accountability purposes.

Britain could have suspended all military intelligence and political links with Israel, including training, joint operations and security cooperation.

Britain could have suspended its trade agreement with Israel and imposed a ban on all settlement products and services.

Britain could have regulated and penalised companies and charities complicit in Israel's unlawful occupation, including investigating UK registered charities raising funds for Israeli military units or settlements.

Britain could have issued wide-reaching, targeted sanctions against senior members of the Israeli political and military establishment responsible for the assault on Gaza and for maintaining the unlawful occupation.

Britain could have prevented British citizens from travelling to Israel to join the Israeli military or participate in military operations in line with obligations under counterterrorism and war crimes legislation.

Britain could have investigated and, where evidence permitted, prosecuted British citizens who have served in the Israeli military and participated in alleged war crimes in Gaza or the OPT under its own laws and the principles of universal jurisdiction.

Britain could have defended the independence of the ICC prosecutor, condemning sanctions against him and his family and providing financial and diplomatic support to protect the court from political interference.

Britain could have supported UN General Assembly and Security Council processes to enforce the ICJ's advisory opinions, including sanctioned suspension of Israel's UN privileges and accountability measures.

Britain could have expanded humanitarian support for Gaza, restoring, increasing and protecting UNRWA to ensure unimpeded humanitarian aid.

Britain could have led international efforts to enforce accountability, including pushing for the execution of ICC warrants and mobilising like-minded states to isolate those obstructing justice.

'Instead,' Tayab Ali said, 'Britain has done precisely the opposite: supplying arms, providing political cover, cutting humanitarian aid, and even undermining the very institutions designed to deliver accountability.' Ali's conclusion was succinct: 'Has Britain fulfilled its legal obligations? The answer is no. Britain has not fulfilled them. Britain has breached them. Britain has chosen complicity over prevention, political expediency over legal duty, and silence over justice.'

Britain could have signed up to the commitments that came out of the Bogotá Emergency Conference for Palestine in July 2025. Convened by the Hague Group and co-chaired by the governments of Colombia and South Africa, the Emergency Conference on Palestine brought together 30 states for two days of intensive deliberation. They emerged with a concrete, coordinated, six-point plan to uphold international law. 'The main objective,' Guillaume Long said, was to move beyond condemning and towards 'concrete state measures in application of international law.' The commitments are 'the kinds of enforcement of international law that the United Kingdom could easily and should absolutely be carrying out in the context of Israel's crimes under international law'.

Britain could have committed to prevent military and dual use exports to Israel. Instead, the UK government refused to impose a comprehensive arms embargo and continued to issue licences for weapons components destined for Israel, weapons which we know are being used in the genocide in Gaza.

Britain could have refused Israeli weapons transfers at their ports. Instead, the UK chose not to cease arms shipments destined for Israel from its ports. Vessels continue to pass freely through UK ports with equipment that we know is being used in the perpetration of war crimes.

Britain could have prevented vessels carrying weapons to Israel under their national flags. The UK has issued no prohibition on UK flag ships carrying arms or fuel to Israel and no measures against vessels complicit in violations of international law.

Britain could have reviewed all public contracts to prevent public institutions and funds from supporting Israel's illegal occupation. Instead, the Conservative government passed legislation in Parliament in June 2023 to restrict public bodies, local authorities and public universities from boycotting companies involved in Israel's illegal occupation. This restriction, which was passed by the previous government, has not been reversed by the Labour government.

Britain could have pursued justice for international crimes. The UK has not initiated a single domestic investigation into or prosecution of war crimes in Gaza.

Britain could have supported universal jurisdiction to hold perpetrators accountable. The UK has not exercised its universal jurisdiction powers to pursue perpetrators of crimes in Gaza.

Guillaume Long, who was a diplomatic advisor to the Hague Group, told the Tribunal:

> The UK is clearly in breach of its obligations under international law, choosing instead to protect its arms industry,

its shipping interests, its political alliances over the lives of Palestinians and its commitments under international law. Other governments have shown the law must and can be enforced through arms embargos, port bans, court rulings, public procurement policies, and international litigation. The law exists. The precedence exists. The mechanisms exist... The UK has chosen instead political convenience over legal obligations.

The desecration of international law

As we have seen from witness testimony, the greatest cost of British complicity in genocide is Palestinian lives. With every witness, the Tribunal revealed that British complicity in genocide has had an immense human cost. As Ali said, 'for Palestinians, Britain's weapons, trade and silence have contributed directly to their suffering and death. Every bomb that falls on Gaza carries with it the shadow of British complicity.' We should never forget that Britain's failure has, above all, cost Palestinian lives, dignity and freedom.

On top of this, Britain's complicity has had an impact on its own standing in the world as a nation allegedly committed to the rule of law in the international arena. 'By ignoring its obligations under international law,' Foreign Minister Long testified, the UK has contributed 'to the erosion of international law [and] the global social contract.' Long highlighted Britain's role as a permanent member of the UN Security Council and as a 'powerful member of the international community', suggesting that with this status come greater responsibilities.

Britain's failure to fulfil its legal obligations has had a

negative impact not merely on the UK's own credibility as an international actor but also on post-Second World War norms, institutions and treaties. By disregarding its obligations under international law, the UK has contributed to the weakening of basic international norms relating to war crimes, crimes against humanity and the duty to ensure that the principle of 'Never Again' be upheld. Ali explained how Britain's failure to uphold its legal obligations 'has emboldened those who seek to dismantle international justice altogether'. Namely, its selective reading of the Genocide Convention has 'stripped it of universality'. Characterising Britain's actions and tactics as 'a complete disregard for both types of scrutiny, judicial and parliamentary', Ó Cuinn said that the government was 'undermining the rule of law'.

Albanese stated that Britain's failure to protect the international rules-based order has 'contributed to this disfigurement and its erosion', putting 'all of us in a situation of fragility and vulnerability to illegality'. In Albanese's words, 'we have entered a phase where might makes right, and none of us has anything to gain from it'.

The horrific experience of the last two and a half years, on top of decades of illegal occupation the Palestinian people have endured, have proved just how weak international law has become, and how the much-vaunted rules-based order is being buried under the rubble along with the Palestinian lives it has failed to protect. If impunity rules the world, then we all face a very grim future. The Gaza Tribunal, yes, is speaking up for the people of Palestine, but it is also speaking up for a world in which everybody – no matter their ethnicity, race or religion – can live in dignity and peace.

Ending the era of impunity

I saw the mortar shell that had gone through the school buildings, the destroyed UN establishments, the burned out schools, the ruined homes, the destroyed lives, the imprisoned people, the psychological damage to a whole generation... This is a war crime that has been undertaken, but this time on live television.

—JEREMY CORBYN, 2010

A two-day Tribunal cannot possibly uncover the full scope and scale of suffering that Palestinians have endured, nor the full scope and scale of British complicity. To this day, we are still denied access to crucial information that the public deserves to know.

That is why we must continue to push for a full, official, independent public inquiry. One that conducts an investigation into any and all cooperation between the UK and Israel since October 2023. One with the power to question current and past ministers and officials involved in decision-making processes. One that enforces a statutory duty of candour on public officials to tell the truth. The government may have thought that, with this Tribunal, we would stop. It is gravely mistaken.

This Tribunal is not a substitute for an independent inquiry. Far from it. This Tribunal, and the evidence it has collated, means the case for an independent inquiry is stronger than ever before. In a similar vein, the government must cooperate with the ICC, ICJ and all other domestic and international mechanisms of accountability, including the independent inquiry named above. More tangibly, that means releasing the full licensing and export data to clarify the nature of military shipments to Israel to date. It means publishing all legal advice regarding the UK government's assessment of genocide and its obligations to prevent it, as well as the legal advice relating to Israel's grave violations of IHL. It means providing the ICC with all surveillance footage it has collected during RAF flights over Gaza.

If we are to change course, we must learn from Britain's profound legal and moral failure. This entails not only changing UK policies to ensure adherence to international law, but also holding accountable those responsible for the UK's complicity with violations of international law and the Genocide Convention. The British government will be aware that the ICC has issued arrest warrants to Israeli officials. The government should therefore be aware that if it knowingly sends weapons to a government whose leader is wanted for war crimes, then it is not immune to the long arm of international law.

The violation of international law could implicate individual ministers and officials, including those who have authorised the continuation of economic ties with Israel, as well as the commission of arms trades, arm transfers and intelligence exchange. Article 4 of the Genocide Convention states that rulers, public officials and private individuals of a country are liable to punishment if they are found to be complicit with genocide. Section 51 of the 2001 International Criminal Court Act notes that genocide, crimes against humanity and war crimes are explicitly set out and incorporated into English law. Tayab Ali agrees: 'For Britain itself, ministers and officials who authorised unlawful exports [and] obstructed accountability risk exposure under universal jurisdiction for themselves.'

We, the authors of *The Gaza Tribunal*, vow to work with domestic and international institutions, including UK cause lawyers, the International Court of Justice and the International Criminal Court, to draw their attention to evidence presented, including violations of international law and of the Genocide Convention and evidence of criminal complicity implicating government ministers and officials.

In the words of Tayab Ali, 'The people of Britain deserve the truth. The people of Palestine deserve justice. And history will judge harshly those who have stood by or, worse, armed and enabled and shielded a genocide. The Tribunal is, therefore, not only an act of truth-telling, but it is also an act of accountability in the face of Britain's profound legal and moral failure.' Britain's actions have implicated its institutions and officials in the gravest breaches of international law. The truth is out. We must not stop – *and we will not stop* – until there is justice for the Palestinian people.

A reckoning is coming

Complicity in genocide cannot be forgotten. It should be prosecuted.
—TAYAB ALI

Palestinians killed waiting for aid in Gaza. In June 2025, 86 Palestinians were shot near 'aid distribution sites'. They came in the hope that they may find a bag of flour. They were mowed down instead. The first time the Israeli military massacred starving Palestinians seeking aid, Israel denied it ever happened. Soon, the almost-daily executions faded into the background. They became part of the total normalisation of unimaginable human suffering. They became part of the daily routine of famine profiteering and genocide.

There is no way to rationalise the horrors that have been inflicted on fellow human beings. It has gone beyond our capacity to mourn, meaningfully, for those whose lives have been erased. Such is the scale of death and destruction that we may never see or hear the stories of those who are buried under the rubble. This was not a battle between one state and another. It may have been couched as an Israeli response to a non-state actor, but in fact it was an affront to Palestinian people wherever they are. What has unfolded is not a conflict of equals, but the systematic starvation, subjugation and destruction of an unarmed civilian population.

As the death toll rose, urgency turned to resignation – and the normalisation of mass death began to pose an ever-greater risk to those whose lives we could have still saved. Human beings continued to be killed: bombed, starved and shot while scrambling for food. Still, the UK government allowed the supply of parts for F-35 jets. Still, the government refused to implement widespread sanctions. Still, the government permitted the use of the RAF base in Akrotiri. Still, our government provided military intelligence. Still, the government provided training to Israeli military personnel. Still, the government failed to fulfil its legal obligations to prevent genocide.

No one can pretend they did not know. Article I of the Genocide Convention makes it very clear: 'the Contracting Parties confirm that genocide, whether committed in time of peace or in time of war, is a crime under international law which they undertake to prevent and to punish.' As early as January 2024, the ICJ recognised a 'plausible risk' that Israel's acts could amount to genocide being committed against the Palestinian people. The president of the ICJ at the time subsequently stated that the purpose was to declare that the

Palestinians had, 'plausible rights to protection from genocide'. In March 2024, the ICJ insisted once more that 'all measures' should be taken to prevent the 'commission of genocidal acts' in Gaza. Thousands of people pursued every avenue to make this government wake up to the horrors it was enabling. These people were ignored, dismissed and demonised. It is utterly shameful that the government wrung its hands while Gaza was continuously pummelled.

We have run out of words to articulate the scale of suffering that has been inflicted upon the people of Gaza. We've heard the most horrendous stories of the position that doctors, health workers and aid workers are placed in. It is almost impossible to imagine what it is like to be a doctor operating on a child without anaesthetic, without even any means of cleaning the wound and just trying to save that life. And if the child survives, the horror that that child has been through will never leave them: the unbelievable levels of pain of an operation without any anaesthetic. And then in some cases, patients have died because there was not enough food, not enough water, not any way of them surviving.

None of this is some act of nature. None of what has transpired is some random event. This is a calculated decision by the Israeli government to deny food, deny water, deny medicine, deny support, deny the opportunity to survive for those that have been injured by the bombs they have dropped. Those young people who've lost their siblings, lost their mum, lost their dad, lost their aunties, uncles, the whole wider family: they will live forever with the survivor's guilt of just still being alive.

Many politicians, having witnessed the annihilation of Gaza and its people, have taken the strategic decision to backtrack on the reality of their unwavering support. If they had any integrity, they would mourn the innocent Palestinian lives that have been erased in the name of self-defence. They should be ashamed of their cowardice, knowing that others have paid the price for the war crimes they refused to oppose. Even now, after Israel's onslaught on Gaza has been translated into a military doctrine which is metastasising in West Asia, they remain silent, knowing full well that they are paving the way for a dystopian future, not just for the Palestinians, but for millions of people all over the world.

CONCLUSION

The Gaza Doctrine

Beyond material contributions to genocide, the UK's governing elite advanced a belief system sympathetic to the extermination of peoples deemed less human. Genocide lies at the heart of any settler-colonial project, and throughout its imperial history the British government was never an innocent bystander. Yet British genocidal acts against Indigenous Australians, Indians, Irish, Kenyans and others were conveniently covered up and erased. This erasure persists today, sustained in part by Britain's dominance in the post-Second World War global order, where accumulated power enables elites to dictate rules, narrate histories and shape perceptions of the present.

This attitude manifests most clearly in Palestine, where the British government supported the Zionist movement's settler-colonial project and later the Israeli colonial state. This served the government's and corporate and media elite's regional interests, perpetuating the fragmentation sown by the 1916 Sykes–Picot Agreement, and later facilitating strategic control over natural resources across the region. Alongside allies, they crafted narratives that justified devaluing Palestinian lives for generations, sentencing millions to alien domination, subjugation, and exploitation and paving the path for an endless saga of violence. These narratives were premised on erasure, denial and the desensitisation of violence.

Even when engaging with international law, the British government pioneered fragmented legal interpretations that undermined the value of equality, as evidenced in its contestation of the ICC's jurisdiction, and actively undermined efforts to enshrine anti-colonial rights in international legal doctrine. In other words, the British ruling elite played a central role in placing Palestinians in the position of what Jill Stauffer coins as 'ethical loneliness', that is, 'the profound experience of being abandoned by humanity, compounded by the cruelty of one's wrongs or suffering not being heard or properly acknowledged when testified to'.

In October 2023, the risk of genocide in Gaza was clear to those who valued Palestinian lives and heeded settler-colonialism's long lessons. As we have shown, British officials possessed the knowledge to foresee this and were provided with ample evidence of Israel's illegal actions as it unleashed unimaginable violence against the Palestinians; the government's failure to abide by its legal obligations under international law and to prevent, in the words of Richard Falk, 'the most transparent genocide in human history' is a continuation of British imperial history. This book demonstrates how the British government wilfully chose complicity in the genocide. This complicity includes military, economic and diplomatic support that fortified Israel's capacity to commit genocide. To sustain a narrative premised on deceit and erasure, dissenting voices inside and outside government were met with suppression, coercion and punishment, with the aid of duplicitous interpretations of the notion 'terrorism' and a definition of anti-semitism that falsely conflates criticism against Israel with anti-Jewish racism.

Despite these efforts, the story of the genocide was told. The violence endured in Gaza was so severe that it pierced every layer of deceptive impunity, and millions of people in the UK and across the globe marched week after week to protest Israel's crimes and their own governments' complicity. Indeed, in the past 32 months, a wide gap has emerged between the ruling elites and the global majority, and the former no longer controls the 'common sense'. Gaza's reality has, moreover, destabilised the post-Second World War international legal order, provoking an existential crisis. The contradictions between lived violence and the positions of powerful states, claiming to uphold international law, sent shockwaves worldwide. The contradictions underscored that the British government is complicit not only in failing to prevent genocide, but also in dismantling the contemporary international legal order and eroding the basic norms it propagates, as affirmed by the UN Special Rapporteur and numerous UN reports. So, what happens when Britian (and other countries) becomes complicit with genocide and allow Israel to act with impunity?

We mentioned the chasm that has emerged between the ruling elite and the people. This rift did not occur spontaneously. The global complicity in the genocide was confronted by a vast movement that had amassed over many years – through incessant labour that included education, training, mobilisation and the creation of alliances among numerous groups with different commitments – and together the people stood in solidarity with Palestine and against the machinations of their own governments. In the UK, the government's effort to criminalise resistance and cast protests supporting self-determination, emancipation and justice as 'hate marches' has been met with fiercer commitment to Palestinian liberation.

Simultaneously, the government's complicity in atrocity crimes has facilitated the normalisation of sadistic violence across the globe. With that, the margin of normalised violence expanded, and unspeakable crimes were desensitised. British complicity formed a central element of the global structure of insulation for atrocity, a world where witnessing shredded human flesh became the daily norm. This is evidenced in the events that took place in June 2025. Amid US–Iranian negotiations aimed at reaching a nuclear deal, Israel started an illegal war, launching wide-scale airstrikes against Iranian military and civilian infrastructures while assassinating senior scientists and military commanders. The United States joined the fray in what is now called the '12-Day War'. Rather than criticising the aggressors, the British government and many of its allies stressed Israel's 'security concerns', once again advancing a narrative in which global peace and security are equated with the perceived interests of the British ruling elites and their allies. The difference between the historical undermining of the 'rules-based order' and now is that the genocidal violence which the British government has supported was streamlined from Gaza and has been naked for all to see, and this shift in the visibility of violence signalled a new phase where publics across the globe could witness the horror.

The people can also see how the erosion of the international legal framework was further precipitated following the so-called ceasefire of October 2025, which in effect allows for the continuation of the genocide in slow motion. The negotiations leading to the ceasefire, or in the words of Ghassan Kanafani, the negotiations between 'the sword and the neck' were premised on coercive abdication of inalienable rights, yet they were repeatedly framed by UK representatives as the only viable path. The coercive and illegal tone of the conversation is evident in the USA and Israel's October 2025 plan for Gaza, that included a US-led so-called 'Board of Peace' and an imposed technocratic administration. This plan effectively negated basic principles like sovereignty, self-determination and accountability. In short, the Board's imagination of the future of Gaza can be described as a dystopic, business-led hyper-technological world premised on the subjugation of the local population. While Palestinian civil society denounced the 'Board of Peace' as a renewed colonial project, the UK government responded by welcoming the proposal even as it decided not to join the Board.

Since the so-called 'ceasefire' entered into force, Israel has killed over 750 people, blocked access to 37 humanitarian organisations and has expropriated 60 per cent of the Gaza Strip, concentrating over 2 million Palestinians in a narrow sliver of land with many of them living in crowded camps with insufficient food and without electricity, running water or a sewage system. Meanwhile, thousands of prisoners suffer unimaginable pain and systemic practices of torture in Israeli prisons. British and European facilitation of this new reality set the stage for lowering the threshold of 'permissible violence' far below that set within the framework of international law, and by so doing further eroded the post-Second World War 'rules-based order'. Sure enough, the USA and Israel did not disappoint.

On 28 February 2026, in the late stages of negotiations to renew a nuclear deal, the USA and Israel launched another illegal war on Iran, which spread quickly to Lebanon and several Gulf countries. Since 2 March 2026, Israel's fighter jets have been relentlessly bombing south Lebanon, Beirut and other cities; this was later followed by a ground incursion and the destruction of dozens of villages and towns in south Lebanon. What we have actually been witnessing is Israel's expansion of its Gaza Doctrine – a combination of mass displacement, mass killing, mass destruction of civilian infrastructure and expropriation of land – to other parts of West Asia.[134] A contemporary iteration of centuries-old mechanisms of colonial accumulation by dispossession, evoking historical images of 'scorched' Irish, Indigenous American and Australian earth. The complicity of Britian and its allies at the height of the genocide in Gaza enabled the doctrine and paved the path for it to metastasise to Iran and even more so to Lebanon.

A grave toll has been exacted on both fronts. Within less than two weeks, more than 4 million civilians had been displaced in the two countries, up to 3.2 million in Iran and more than 1 million in Lebanon, where Israel had issued evacuation orders that cover 14 per cent of the country's territory. Evidence suggests that such blanket evacuation orders alongside the destruction of villages and the establishment of military outposts mask the intention of the ethnic cleansing of the south of Lebanon. The total death toll is in the thousands, with tens of thousands more injured.

In Iran, the Red Crescent reported that more than 125,000 civilian sites have been damaged or destroyed by 10 April 2026, including around 100,000 residential properties and 23,500 commercial buildings. Among these sites are a disturbingly high number of medical centres. This is not surprising considering that one of the more pronounced features of the Gaza Doctrine is turning lifesaving medical sites like hospitals, health clinics and ambulances into targets: it was the 'deliberate and systematic dismantling of Gaza's health and life-sustaining systems' that Physicians for Human Rights Israel (PHRI) cited to argue that the Israeli military's conduct in the Strip met the legal definition of genocide. The reports emerging out of Iran and Lebanon raise the deeply troubling prospect that Israel hopes to replicate that 'success' abroad.

The Iranian Red Crescent reports that US–Israeli strikes have, at the time of writing, damaged 39 medical facilities – including hospitals, pharmacies, laboratories, health centres and emergency units – with some rendered inoperable and others resuming partial operations. On the war's second day, airstrikes did significant damage to the Gandhi Hospital in Tehran, where footage and photographs showed the building's blown-out, debris-strewn façade and broken equipment and shattered glass inside the wards. The head of Iran's medical council, Mohammad Raeiszadeh, disclosed on state media that the strike disabled the hospital's *in vitro* fertilisation department; witnesses told the television network Al-Alam that newborn infants and other patients had to be evacuated.

In Lebanon, health infrastructure appears to be under still more direct attack. On Friday, 13 March 2026, nearly two weeks into the Lebanese front of 'Operation Roaring Lion', Israeli forces bombed Burj Qalaouiyah, a village in the country's south. The strike destroyed a healthcare centre, killing twelve doctors, paramedics, nurses and patients; the *New York Times* reported that 'only one severely injured worker survived'. Among the victims, according to the journalist Lylla Younes's reporting for Drop Site, was a paramedic who had spoken last fall at a memorial service for several colleagues killed by an Israeli airstrike during the previous war in Lebanon. 'Even if we are killed one by one,' he reportedly said then, 'we will not abandon our duty.'

Two days before the strike on the medical centre in Burj Qalaouiyah, the World Health Organization (WHO) had already confirmed that services have shrunk even as the need for medical care intensifies.[135] The attacks on health care seem designed to encourage the mass displacement: in an interview with the *Guardian*, an emergency worker called them part of a campaign 'to prevent life in our region and push people to flee'.[136] As of 17 April 2026, Israel has killed over 90 healthcare workers in Lebanon and wounded over 200 more.

The harm generated by these strikes reverberates broadly. Ever since March 2025, when Israel demolished the Turkish–Palestinian Friendship Hospital, the only cancer hospital in Gaza, the 10,000 patients the facility treated each year simply have had nowhere to go. 'To have cancer in Gaza means death, and before death, it means a lot of suffering and pain,' the Palestinian oncologist Sobhi Skaik told *The Lancet Oncology*.[137] Since an additional 2,000 to 2,500 people in Gaza are diagnosed with cancer annually, the hospital's destruction will undoubtedly cause thousands of excess deaths in the years to come.

The statistics about the attacks on Iran and Lebanon's medical systems index a range of violations. Already on 6 March the head spokesperson for Iran's health ministry reported that the US–Israeli strikes had put nine hospitals out of service, destroyed more than a dozen 'pre-hospital emergency bases', and damaged multiple local-level and rural health facilities.[138] The *Guardian* reported that since 2 March Israel has carried out multiple 'double-tap' strikes, whereby an initial strike is followed by a pause during which first responders often arrive, before the area is bombed again. This tactic likely violates Common Article 3 of the Geneva Conventions of 1949, which prohibits targeting civilians, the wounded, or those placed *hors de combat*.

When pressed about these attacks on medical facilities and other civilian infrastructure, Israel and the USA have repeatedly reached for responses out of the Gaza playbook, which seeks to sow distortion and confusion in the public discussion on the subject matter. After a strike killed 175 people, most of them young children, at a girls' school in southern Iran on the first day of the war, President Trump denied responsibility, suggesting to reporters as late as 7 March that an Iranian missile had misfired. On 11 March 2026, the *New York Times* reported that an ongoing military investigation had made a preliminary finding that the school was hit by a US Tomahawk missile.[139] The previous day, in a press briefing, US defence secretary Pete Hegseth had accused Iran of 'moving rocket launchers into civilian neighbourhoods near schools, near hospitals to try to prevent our ability to strike. That's how they operate... They target civilians. We do not'.

The Israeli and American narrative relies on the blanket demonisation of any expression of Palestinian, Lebanese or Iranian resistance. This narrative conveniently erases an indisputable fact: in all these contexts, Israel and the USA are the aggressors seeking to dominate, subjugate and exploit the peoples of West Asia.

Denying well-substantiated allegations of crimes: these are preludes to the still more radical step of discarding the international legal framework. Perhaps the most telling development in the current war is that Israel and the USA have not even bothered to justify bombing civilian infrastructure. 'No quarter, no mercy,' Hegseth said in a press conference on 13 March, echoing President Trump's infamous assertion, following the illegal abduction of Venezuelan President Nicolás Maduro, that 'I don't need international law.' Israel, surprisingly or not, has embraced the crimes it perpetrated, dropping leaflets on Beirut reminding the city's residents of the Israeli military's 'great success in Gaza'. Referring to Israel's attacks on Iran and Lebanon, Benjamin Netanyahu explained on 12 March that the 'dramatic shift in our power relative to the power of our enemies is the key to ensuring our existence. Threats come and go – but when we become a regional power, and in certain fields a global power, we have the strength to push dangers away from us and secure our future.'[140] The terms 'law' and 'legal order' were not mentioned once.

These are the words of men drunk on their own power. The Gaza Doctrine is a direct reflection of this intoxication, and the wholesale destruction of health facilities is just one of its manifestations. Moreover, the Gaza Doctrine is a symptom of tectonic shifts in the global world order. It reflects the decay of hegemonic powers that exert maximum force in a desperate attempt to salvage their dominance. Historically, those most precarious bore the wounds of dying empires intent on scorching the land before their inevitable departure.

As the current US–Israeli war and the expansion of the Gaza Doctrine to other areas in West Asia erodes the post-Second World War international order still further, Keir Starmer's government decided to close the Foreign Office unit tracking Israel's potential breaches of international law, thus further contributing to the grinding down of international norms aimed at limiting war and protecting civilians and civilian sites. We need to urgently consider what new tools we can develop to protect the world from spineless politicians who care only about their political survival and men for whom only might makes right. One obvious place to begin is by committing ourselves to solidarity with those who are relentlessly targeted and uniting our voices and protecting those who are prosecuted for speaking out. Only through collective work anchored in the ideals of justice and a clear-sighted perception that pierces the veil of power-laden, distortive narratives can we challenge the repetition of Gaza's story. As we move forward, we must acknowledge that the world order is changing, and we must respond accordingly. This change signals new opportunities for dissent, but also higher risks of cementing new forms of domination exemplified in the Gaza Doctrine.

At this historical juncture, we must revive international legal principles on decolonisation and structural economic equality, establishing the negation of foreign domination, subjugation and exploitation as the pillars of international peace and security. This revival comes with a clear reckoning with the histories of imperial domination and the reversal of historical erasure. By finding our common lexicon and through collective organising, we can break away from 'learned helplessness' and challenge the devaluation of human life through the popularisation of the 'Gaza Doctrine' mentality.

To speak of peace, we must speak of justice. To speak of justice, we must see reality from the standpoint of those most precarious, past and present.

We accordingly place this document in the hands of the British and international public, calling on them to join our cry of 'Never again, for everyone.' We hope it serves as a historical mirror, evoking warnings from centuries of accumulated violence. We hope it triggers accountability in the present and endures as an antidote to colonial erasure in the future.

Afterword

Sally Rooney

The genocide in Gaza marks a newly devastating chapter in the ongoing history of violence against the Palestinian people. Since 2023, many of us looking on from Europe and elsewhere have felt powerless in the face of such horror. Our own nation states, our own elected officials, have plainly failed in their duties to prevent genocide. But it has not always been clear to us what exactly this failure consists of. After all, the conflict is taking place far outside our borders. There seems to be no simple lever that states can pull to make the appalling violence stop. Some of our leaders have even made sympathetic-sounding statements about human rights and international law. Mainstream media outlets do not, by and large, make it clear what else our governments should or even could really be doing. Still, we suspect, our political leadership must somehow be failing to act.

In that suspicion, we are wrong. What this Tribunal establishes beyond any doubt is that the United Kingdom has not failed to act. On the contrary: the British government has taken decisive action, committing significant military, political, diplomatic and economic resources to facilitating the genocide in Gaza. As this book attests, the UK has provided weapons for use in the mass killing of civilians; conducted surveillance flights over Gaza and shared the resulting intelligence with the Israeli military; helped to train Israeli army officers; provided visiting Israeli military figures with special immunity from arrest; publicly defended the forced starvation of millions of civilians; actively worked to block and undermine the international legal system in order to protect Israel from accountability; and more.

In this complicity, the UK government has been acting not at the behest of its electorate, but rather in the face of sustained public outcry. Polls show that almost two-thirds of British people favour a full embargo on arms trade with Israel. Hundreds of thousands of people have taken to the streets in what the *Guardian* has described as 'the biggest UK protest movement in recent history'. As in the anti-war movement in 2003, some have even felt called to take direct action, trying to disrupt the military supply chain by sabotaging arms factories, planes and weapons. In response, the UK government has distanced itself not from the Israeli state but from the British public, taking extraordinary measures to criminalise peaceful protest, curtail freedom of speech and treat civil disobedience as terrorism.

Britain's involvement in the genocide began under a Conservative administration and has continued uninterrupted under the present Labour government. In the face of mass public opposition, the two parties have colluded to deprive the British electorate of any influence over UK–Israeli relations. Elections have been arranged so as to offer no alternative. Non-disruptive protests have been ignored. Disruptive protests have been harshly criminalised. And even now, complicity continues. The genocide in Gaza has both revealed and intensified the deterioration of democratic life in Britain. If that decline is not halted – if the ruling parties face no consequences for collaborating against the public and outlawing dissent – then it will leach into every aspect of public life. Democracy itself is at stake.

This book establishes the distinctive role the UK has played in facilitating war crimes in Gaza. But in a broader sense, the Tribunal also speaks to the vital integration of the Israeli state within a wide network of international support. At the time of writing, for instance, every European nation is in violation of at least some of its international duties under the Genocide Convention, including purported allies of Palestine like Ireland. Inquiries like this one are crucial in establishing the extent and nature of state complicity and communicating these important facts to the public. The UK's Gaza Tribunal should serve as a starting point not only for national reckoning in Britain but also for public investigation and accountability elsewhere.

The calculation that has led so many wealthy nations around the world to facilitate genocide has ultimately been a political one. In the case of the UK's illegal provision of military parts for Israeli fighter planes, this book makes it clear: the 'real reason' for the continued supply is 'the lack of political will to confront the United States'. Israel itself is ultimately a small, aggressive and diplomatically toxic nation in the Middle East; only in its capacity as a projection of US power does it command such extraordinary international support. The lack of political will throughout Europe and elsewhere to confront the United States is, of course, a kind of cowardice, but a calculated kind. Currying favour with a global superpower, while perhaps humiliating, is supposed to reap rewards. And in pursuit of those rewards, states all over the world have chosen not only to overlook but often to participate in genocide.

Having betrayed their own people and made a mockery of international law, what exactly do countries like the UK have to show for it? An Israeli regime emboldened by international complicity has invaded Lebanon, killing thousands and displacing over a million people. Meanwhile, the US–Israeli partnership has waged an illegal war on Iran, resulting in the closure of the Strait of Hormuz and a catastrophic global energy crisis. States like the United Kingdom – having obediently facilitated atrocity crimes in order to ingratiate themselves with the USA – are now facing economic chaos at home as well as an uncontrollable spiral of violence in the Middle East. Europe's inexpressibly gruesome wager has been a losing one, and we have not even begun to reckon with the cost.

Palestine may represent the tightest point of contradiction in the world geopolitical system. The intrinsic violence of imperial relations – elsewhere often spatially dispersed and devolved through non-state corporations and agencies – is laid bare for the world to see. And just as the question of Palestine reveals, like no other, the chasm between public opinion and state activity in the Global North, so it also reveals the immeasurable abyss between the institutions of international law and the geopolitical reality of apartheid, torture, displacement, assassination and genocide. These contradictions, at their most asphyxiating in Palestine, are now tightening everywhere. The fragility of world food systems, the overpowering political dominance of the military and fossil fuel industries, the soaring inequalities that have eroded community life, the collapse of effective labour organising, and the proximity of complete climate breakdown: these are among the realities that have enabled and escalated a live-streamed genocide. Gaza forces us to confront them not in a distant image of the future but here and now.

In a letter-essay written during his extended imprisonment, the novelist Walid Daqqa invoked the idea of 'Parallel Time' to describe the experience of Palestinian prisoners: 'we, in Parallel Time, see you, while you all do not see us… We are a past continuous and never-ending. We address you all from it presently, so that it does not become your future.' Gaza today is perhaps the 'Parallel Time' of all civilisation, seeing and unseen, past and never-ending. To see Gaza – not as a tragic historical event, not as a list of facts and statistics, but as a really existing place at this moment – is to enter a different relationship with the future.

'I profess that my heart skips a beat at the sight of a flower on the television, at a scene of nature, at the sea,' Daqqa wrote after almost 20 years in prison. 'I profess that I am joyous despite it all…' Gaza has long been an open-air prison, and it has now become a mass grave, yes. But it is also home to millions of living and beloved Palestinian people. In seeing Gaza as it is now, we must see that life itself is something indescribably precious: that even one moment of life, a single instant of living consciousness, is infinitely and irreplaceably beautiful. And we must be prepared to fight for it: for the lives of the living, for our future, and for a free Palestine.

Authors

JEREMY CORBYN has been the MP for Islington North since 1983 and is the former leader of the Labour Party. He is currently Vice-President of the *Campaign for Nuclear Disarmament*, Acting Deputy President of the *Stop the War Coalition*, Patron of the *Palestine Solidarity Campaign* and a Cabinet Member of *Progressive International*. In 2020, Jeremy Corbyn founded the Peace and Justice Project, bringing people together for social and economic justice, peace and human rights in Britain and across the world.

NEVE GORDON is a professor at the School of Law at Queen Mary, University of London and a Fellow of the British Academy of Social Sciences. He is the author of *Israel's Occupation* and co-author of *The Human Right to Dominate, and Human Shields: A History of People in the Line of Fire*, reprinted in paperback in 2026 with a new preface and epilogue about Gaza.

SHAHD HAMMOURI is an academic and international lawyer specialising in corporate war profiteering, self-determination and critical legal theory. She is the author of *Corporate War Profiteering and International Law* and serves as a senior legal consultant at Law for Palestine and a Lecturer in International Law and legal theory at the University of Kent.

SALLY ROONEY is the author of four novels, most recently *Intermezzo*, as well as a range of literary and cultural criticism. Her work is widely translated and internationally acclaimed. She has been affiliated with the Palestinian Campaign for the Academic and Cultural Boycott of Israel since 2021. In 2022, she was named among *Time* magazine's 100 most influential people in the world. She lives and works in her home county of Mayo, in the west of Ireland.

Witnesses

ABUBAKER ABED is a Palestinian journalist, writer and translator from Deir al-Balah Refugee Camp in Gaza. Abed was forced to flee Gaza in 2025 and now lives in Dublin, Ireland.

TAREQ ABU AZZOUM is a journalist who was born and raised in Gaza City. He is currently a correspondent for Al Jazeera.

FRANCESCA ALBANESE is an international lawyer, specialising in human rights and the Middle East. Since May 2022, she has served as the United Nations Special Rapporteur on the Occupied Palestinian Territories.

TAYAB ALI is the Director of the International Centre of Justice for Palestinians. As head of Bindmans' Crime and Extradition teams, and International Law team, Ali is an internationally recognised solicitor advocate, and is one of the UK's leading criminal and international law specialists.

CHARLOTTE ANDREWS-BRISCOE is a lawyer with the Global Legal Action Network (GLAN) and a consultant at Bindmans

LLP. Andrews-Briscoe works on GLAN's public law litigation, both domestically and internationally, particularly with respect to the prevention of the commission of war crimes, and accountability thereafter. She is a member of the legal team representing Al-Haq in *Al Haq* v *Secretary of State for Business and Trade*, which is challenging the UK government's decision to grant export licences for arms sales to Israel.

PEDRO ARROJO-AGUDO is the Special Rapporteur on the human rights to safe drinking water and sanitation. Previously, from 2016 to 2019, Arrojo-Agudo served as an elected member (MP) of the Spanish Parliament during its eleventh and twelfth legislature, during which he was part of the International Cooperation Committee working on human rights.

RICHARD BURGON has been the Member of Parliament for Leeds East since 2015. Under Jeremy Corbyn's leadership, Burgon served as Shadow Secretary of State for Justice and Shadow Lord Chancellor from 2016 to 2020.

RICHARD FALK is Albert G. Milbank Professor of International Law and Practice, Emeritus at Princeton University, and was Visiting Distinguished Professor in Global and International Studies at the University of California, Santa Barbara (2001–2004). Falk served as the UN Special Rapporteur on Palestinian human rights from 2008 to 2014.

KATIE FALLON is advocacy manager at the Campaign Against Arms Trade, where she leads CAAT's parliamentary and legal advocacy, including as part of the campaign for an arms embargo on UK exports to Israel.

PAULA GAVIRIA BETANCUR is a human rights lawyer and a forced displacement expert. She currently serves as executive director of Compaz, a non-profit founded by Nobel Laureate Juan Manuel Santos. In September 2022, she was appointed as the United Nations Special Rapporteur on the human rights of internally displaced persons.

JEFF HALPER is an Israeli anthropologist, the Director of the Israeli Committee Against House Demolitions (ICAHD) and a member of the One Democratic State Campaign. His latest book is *Decolonizing Israel, Liberating Palestine: Zionism, Settler Colonialism and the Case for One Democratic State* (London: Pluto, 2021).

FRAN HEATHCOTE is a British trade unionist and the current General Secretary of the Public and Commercial Services Union (PCS). She was the first woman to hold this position.

SARA HUSSEINI is the Director of the British Palestinian Council, an independent voice on British policy towards Palestine. She has previously served as an advisor to senior PLO officials, including the former Secretary General and the Palestinian Ambassador to Germany.

BEN JAMAL is the director of the Palestine Solidarity Campaign (PSC). His father's family was driven out of Jerusalem and into exile during the Nakba in 1948. Ben was the first Palestinian to be appointed as the Director of PSC.

MATT KENNARD is an investigative journalist who co-founded *Declassified UK*. He formerly worked as director at the Centre for Investigative Journalism (CIJ) in London and as a staff writer for the *Financial Times*.

FORZ KHAN is a leading senior barrister and operates from the Chambers of F Khan in London. He was a lawyer for the family of James Henderson, a British aid worker who was killed in Gaza in an Israeli attack in April 2024.

RAMI KHAYAL is an activist from the Palestinian Youth Movement, a grassroots, international movement that organises Palestinian and Arab youth to struggle for Palestinian liberation.

GUILLAUME LONG served as Foreign Minister of Ecuador under the government of Rafael Correa and was the country's Permanent Representative to the United Nations until January 2018. He is a senior policy analyst at the Center for Economic Policy and Research (CEPR). In addition, he is diplomatic advisor in the Hague Group, the coalition of countries that is taking measures to confront the genocide in Gaza.

JOHN MCEVOY is Chief Reporter for *Declassified UK*. John is a historian and filmmaker whose work focuses on British foreign policy and Latin America.

NICK MAYNARD is a leading consultant surgeon and professor based in Oxford. Professor Maynard has worked extensively in Gaza since 2010, teaching medical students and carrying out upper GI surgery. He has travelled out to Gaza regularly since October 2023 to provide humanitarian aid.

GEARÓID Ó CUINN is the founding director of the Global Legal Action Network (GLAN) where he is responsible for GLAN's legal actions and strategic growth. He is an adjunct lecturer at the Irish Centre for Human Rights and formerly lectured at Lancaster University Law School and was a visiting fellow at the Transnational Law Institute at Kings College London.

NATALIE ROBERTS is the Executive Director of Médecins Sans Frontières/Doctors Without Borders (MSF) in the UK. A British emergency doctor, Roberts joined MSF in 2012 and subsequently held emergency coordination roles in zones of conflict and crisis across Africa, Asia and the Middle East, including in Syria, Yemen, Ukraine, Pakistan, the Philippines, Ethiopia and the Central African Republic.

VICTORIA ROSE is a consultant plastic surgeon at Guy's and St Thomas' NHS Foundation Trust and King's College Hospital NHS Foundation Trust. Dr Rose first joined missions to Gaza through the charity IDEALS in 2019, where she contributed to the development and training of Gaza's limb reconstruction specialists. Since 2024, she has undertaken multiple humanitarian missions in Gaza.

HALA SABBAH is a Palestinian who has lived in the Gulf, Algeria, Jordan and the UK, where she is currently based. She is the co-founder of The Sameer Project, Palestinian led mutual aid group.

RAZ SEGAL is Associate Professor of Holocaust and Genocide Studies and Endowed Professor in the Study of Modern

Genocide at Stockton University, where he also serves as Director of the MA programme in Holocaust and Genocide Studies.

MARK SMITH was a British Foreign Office official who resigned in protest over continued arms sales to Israel in August 2024. Smith was the lead official on the UK arms export licensing report, which assessed whether the UK was legally compliant.

NICOS TRIMIKLINIOTIS is Professor of Sociology, Social Sciences and Law, at the School of Humanities and Social Sciences, University of Nicosia. He heads the team of experts of the Cyprus team for the Fundamental Rights Agency of the EU. He is also an Associate Tenant at Garden Court Chambers.

EMILY TRIPP is the Executive Director of Airwars. From 2021, she worked as the Research Manager, and took over the leadership of the organisation in June 2022 from founder and former director Chris Woods. Her previous experience includes working in humanitarian aid delivery in the Middle East, with a focus on carrying out research and managing assessment teams in Syria and Libya to help inform humanitarian responses.

EYAL WEIZMAN is Professor of Spatial and Visual Cultures and founding director of the Centre for Research Architecture at Goldsmiths, University of London. In 2010, he founded the research agency Forensic Architecture and has directed it ever since.

RALPH WILDE is a professor in the Faculty of Laws at

University College London. Ralph previously served on the Executive Board of the European Society of International Law, the Executive Council of the American Society of International Law, and at the International Law Association (ILA) as Co-Rapporteur of the Human Rights Committee, one of the UK representatives on the international Executive Council, Rapporteur of the Study Group on UN Reform, and Joint Honorary Secretary of the British Branch.

Acknowledgements

We owe an enormous debt to many people for making *The Gaza Tribunal* happen.

Above all, thank you to all of the witnesses – Nick Maynard, Hala Sabbah, Abubaker Abed, Victoria Rose, Jeff Halper, Emily Tripp, Natalie Roberts, Ben Jamal, Tareq Abu Azzoum, Francesca Albanese, Ralph Wilde, Paula Gaviria Betancur, Pedro Arrojo-Agudo, Katie Fallon, Richard Burgon MP, John McEvoy, Charlotte Andrews-Briscoe, Nicos Trimikliniotis, Matt Kennard, Forz Khan, Mark Smith, Fran Heathcote, Sara Husseini, Eyal Weizman, Richard Falk, Rami Khayal, Guillaume Long, Raz Segal, Gearóid Ó Cuinn and Tayab Ali – for giving up your time to testify at the Gaza Tribunal. Your courage, resilience and commitment to justice is a true inspiration to us all.

This book would simply not have been possible without Oly Durose, whose continued work and support has been indispensable from beginning to end, and whose initial idea to launch an inquiry into British complicity became the foundation for *The Gaza Tribunal.*

We would like to thank Artin Giles for your dedication in helping to plan and coordinate the Tribunal, for managing the complex logistics, and for your essential assistance in the production of the original report. We are also extremely grateful to Lori Allen, Matthew Pearce, Mercedes May Hildreth, James Schneider, Samuel Sweek, Sinéad Carroll and Dimitri Van Den Meerssche for your invaluable research, work and support.

Thank you to all those named above, alongside Miriam Stewart, Richard Baldwin, Laura Alvarez, Cai Finch, Ezzideen Abou-Daya and Carmel Kittana, for your help in running the Tribunal. The event would not have been possible without all the staff at Church House. Thank you to all the staff at the Peace and Justice Project – Artin, Sam, Sinéad, Stephanie Linkogle, Karie Murphy and Marion Roberts – for the work you do and will continue to do.

We are immensely grateful to David Castle, Jamie Bowman, Chris Browne and Jonila Krasniqi at Pluto Books for publishing this important work. Thank you to Thérèse Wassily Saba for your meticulous and thoughtful editing, and to Melanie Patrick for producing the stunning cover for this book.

Thank you to Sally Rooney, not just for your profoundly moving afterword, but for the courage you have shown in speaking up for the Palestinian people. Your moral integrity is rare – and it does not go unnoticed. Thank you for standing with Palestine while the world looks away.

Finally, we want to thank every single person who has demonstrated and campaigned against Britain's complicity in genocide. History will remember that you stood up for our common humanity in the face of the greatest crime of our time.

Notes

Preface

1. Gaza (Independent Public Inquiry) Bill, *Hansard*, https://bills.parliament.uk/bills/3987, last updated 25 February 2026.

Introduction

2. United Nations, 'Palestine: UN Rights Chief Highlights Suffering, Atrocity Crimes "that Remain Unpunished"', *UN News*, 26 February 2026, https://news.un.org/en/story/2026/02/1167043.
3. The Palestine Institute for Public Diplomacy, 'Palestinian Civil Society on Trump's "Peace Plan"', 2 October 2025, www.thepipd.com/statements/palestinian-civil-society-on-trumps-peace-plan/

Chapter 1: In Defiance of Illusions

4. Aimé Césaire, *Discourse on Colonialism* (New York: Monthly Review Press, 2000).

5. Ali Kadri, *The Accumulation of Waste: A Political Economy of Systemic Destruction* (Boston, MA: Brill, 2023).
6. Samir Amin, *Empire of Chaos* (New York: Monthly Review Press, 1992).
7. Omar El Akkad, *One Day, Everyone Will Have Always Been Against This* (Edinburgh: Canongate Books, 2025).

Chapter 3: Genocide

8. United Nations, 'More Than 38,000 Women and Girls Killed in Gaza War, UN Gender Equality Agency reports', *UN News*, 17 April 2026, https://news.un.org/en/story/2026/04/1167319.
9. Samuel Granados et al., 'Two Months After Cease-Fire, Israel Is Still Demolishing Gaza', *New York Times*, 12 January 2026, www.nytimes.com/interactive/2026/01/12/world/middleeast/israel-cease-fire-gaza-demolition.html; and UNICEF, 'Rebuilding Hope: UNICEF Expands "Back to Learning" for Hundreds of Thousands of Children in Gaza', 27 January 2026, www.unicef.org/press-releases/rebuilding-hope-unicef-expands-back-learning-hundreds-thousands-children-gaza.
10. 'More Than 95 Percent of Gaza's Agricultural Land Unusable, UN Warns', *Al Jazeera*, 26 May 2025, www.aljazeera.com/news/2025/5/26/more-than-95-percent-of-gazas-agricultural-land-unusable-un-warns.
11. UNRWA, 'Situation Report 184 on the Humanitarian Crisis in the Gaza Strip and the Occupied West Bank, including East Jerusalem', 15 August 2025, www.un.org/unispal/document/unrwa-sitrep-184-15aug25/.
12. United Nations, 'The Question of Palestine: Origins and Evolution of the Palestine Problem: 1917–1947 (Part 1)', www.

un.org/unispal/history2/origins-and-evolution-of-the-palestine-problem/part-i-1917-1947/; and Noura Erakat, *Justice for Some: Law and the Question of Palestine* (Stanford, CA: Stanford University Press, 2020).

13. Jacob Norris, 'Repression and Rebellion: Britain's Response to the Arab Revolt in Palestine of 1936–39', *The Journal of Imperial and Commonwealth History* 36, no. 1 (2008): 25–45.

14. Ahmad H. Sa'di and Lila Abu-Lughod, eds., *Nakba: Palestine, 1948, and the Claims of Memory* (New York: Columbia University Press, 2007), 3–5, 295.

15. Alexander Kedar and Oren Yiftachel, 'Land Regime and Social Relations in Israel', in *Realizing Property Rights*, ed. Hernando de Soto and Francis Cheneval, *Swiss Human Rights Book, Vol. 1* (Zurich: Rüffer and Rub, 2006), 137.

16. Jean-Pierre Filiu, *Gaza: A History*, translated by John King (Oxford: Oxford University Press, 2014), 71 and 195.

17. Neve Gordon, *Israel's Occupation* (Berkeley, CA: University of California Press, 2008).

18. Neve Gordon and Muna Haddad, 'The Road to Famine in Gaza', *New York Review of Books*, 30 March 2024, 1, www.nybooks.com/online/2024/03/30/the-road-to-famine-in-gaza/.

19. International Court of Justice, 'Summary of the Advisory Opinion of 19 July 2024', 19 July 2024, www.icj-cij.org/node/204176.

20. Independent International Commission of Inquiry on the Occupied Palestinian Territory, including East Jerusalem, and Israel, 'Detailed Findings on Attacks Carried Out On and after 7 October 2023 in Israel', UN Doc. A/HRC/56/CRP.3, 10 June 2024, paras. 223–233, www.ohchr.org/sites/default/files/documents/hrbodies/hrcouncil/sessions-regular/session56/a-hrc-56-crp-3.pdf.

21. Daris Widya Saskara, Polly Wilson and Iain Overton, 'Why Did Britain's Arms Licensing Regime to Israel Ignore the Genocidal Language by Israel's Leadership?' Action on Armed Violence, 19 January 2026, https://aoav.org.uk/2026/why-did-britains-arms-licensing-regime-to-israel-ignore-the-genocidal-language-by-israels-leadership/.
22. Amnesty International, 'Global: Social Media Companies Must Step Up Crisis Response on Israel-Palestine as Online Hate and Censorship Proliferate', 27 October 2023, www.amnesty.org/en/latest/news/2023/10/global-social-media-companies-must-step-up-crisis-response-on-israel-palestine-as-online-hate-and-censorship-proliferate/.
23. Israel Ministry of Foreign Affairs, 'Statement by PM Netanyahu', 18 October 2023, gov.il, www.gov.il/en/pages/pm-netanyahu-statement-18-oct-2023.
24. Parallel Parliament, 'Israel and Gaza: Rishi Sunak Excerpts', 16 October 2023, https://parallelparliament.co.uk/mp/rishi-sunak/debate/2023-10-16/commons/commons-chamber/israel-and-gaza.
25. MEE Staff, 'Israel–Palestine War: Keir Starmer Supports Israel's "Right" to Cut Gaza's Water and Power', *Middle East Eye*, 11 October 2023, www.middleeasteye.net/news/israel-palestine-war-keir-starmer-criticised-right-cut-gaza-water-power.
26. International Committee of the Red Cross, 'Amendment to Article 8 of the Rome Statute of the International Criminal Court (Starvation of Civilians as a Method of Warfare)', https://ihl-databases.icrc.org/en/ihl-treaties/icc-statute-amendment-art8-starvation-2019.
27. Patrick Kingsley, Isabel Kershner and Edward Wong, 'Israel and Hamas Step Up Rhetoric as Fighting Rages', *New York Times*, 15 November 2023, www.nytimes.com/2023/11/15/

world/middleeast/israel-gaza-war-rhetoric.html; and Palestine Chronicle Staff, '"Biblical Vengeance": Israeli Politician Wants to Turn Gaza into Dresden', *The Palestine Chronicle*, 25 October 2023, www.palestinechronicle.com/biblical-vengeance-israeli-politician-wants-to-turn-gaza-to-dresden.

28. The Wire Staff, 'Northern Gaza, Israel–Palestine Conflict', *The Wire*, 14 October 2023, https://thewire.in/world/northern-gaza-israel-palestine-conflict.

29. David Gritten and Imogen Foulkes, 'Israel Has Committed Genocide in Gaza, UN Commission of Inquiry Says', *BBC News*, 16 September 2025, www.bbc.co.uk/news/articles/c8641wvon4go; and Israel Ministry of Foreign Affairs, 'Excerpt from PM Netanyahu's Remarks at the Opening of the Winter Assembly of the 25th Knesset's Second Session', 16 October 2023, gov.il, www.gov.il/en/pages/excerpt-from-pm-netanyahu-s-remarks-at-the-opening-of-the-knesset-s-winter-assembly-16-oct-2023.

30. 'Satellite Data Shows at Least 70 Percent of Gaza Buildings Leveled', *Haaretz*, 17 July 2025, www.haaretz.com/israel-news/2025-07-17/ty-article-magazine/.premium/satellite-data-shows-at-least-70-percent-of-gaza-buildings-leveled/00000198-12de-d9c7-af98-7adffc8f00c0.

31. 'Israeli Military's Own Data Indicates Civilian Death Rate of 83% in Gaza War', *Guardian*, 21 August 2025, www.theguardian.com/world/ng-interactive/2025/aug/21/revealed-israeli-militarys-own-data-indicates-civilian-death-rate-of-83-in-gaza-war.

32. UNRWA, *Situation Report 184*, 15 August 2025, www.un.org/unispal/document/unrwa-sitrep-184-15aug25/.

33. Nicola Perugini and Neve Gordon. '"Medicide" in Gaza and International Law: Time for Banning the Bombing of Hos-

pitals', *Institute for Palestine Studies* 94, 10 September 2024, www.palestine-studies.org/en/node/1656099.
34. Rushdi Abu Alouf and George Wright, 'Gaza Hospitals Risk Turning into Morgues, Red Cross Says', *BBC News*, 12 October 2023, www.bbc.co.uk/news/world-middle-east-67087035.amp.
35. Abu Alouf and Wright, 'Gaza Hospitals Risk Turning into Morgues'.
36. Simmone Shah, 'The Gaza Healthcare System Is Reportedly on the Brink of Collapse', *Time*, 24 October 2023, https://time.com/6328038/gaza-healthcare-system-collapse-fuel-hospital/.
37. Shah, 'The Gaza Healthcare System'; and Handicap International: Humanity and Inclusion, 'Attacks on Healthcare and Impacts on Physical Rehabilitation and Mental Health Services in the Gaza Strip', November 2023, www.humanity-inclusion.org.uk/sn_uploads/document/202311-Issue-Brief-Gaza-Health-Rehabilitation-EN.pdf.
38. Francesca Albanese, *Anatomy of a Genocide: Report of the Special Rapporteur on the Situation of Human Rights in the Palestinian Territories Occupied since 1967*, UN Doc. A/HRC/55/73, 1 July 2024), 2, 22–24, https://docs.un.org/en/A/HRC/55/73; Maarten van der Heijden, 'The Well-Worn Playbook for Bombing Hospitals in War: Deny, Deflect, Justify', *Guardian*, 26 February 2025, www.theguardian.com/global-development/2025/feb/26/the-well-worn-playbook-for-bombing-hospitals-in-war-deny-deflect-justify-time-for-the-law-to-close-these-loopholes.
39. Nicola Perugini and Neve Gordon, 'Medical Lawfare: The Nakba and Israel's Attacks on Palestinian Healthcare', *Journal of Palestine Studies* 53, no.1 (2024):68–91, https://doi.org/10.1080/0377919X.2024.2330366.

40. Independent International Commission of Inquiry on the Occupied Palestinian Territory, including East Jerusalem and Israel, *Detailed Findings on the Military Operations and Attacks Carried out in the Occupied Palestinian Territory from 7 October to 31 December 2023*, UN Doc. A/HRC/56/CRP.4, 10 June 2024, 62, https://digitallibrary.un.org/record/4051249?ln=en&v=pdf.
41. B'Tselem: The Israeli Information Center for Human Rights in the Occupied Territories, *Our Genocide*, July 2025, 35–39, www.btselem.org/publications/202507_our_genocide.
42. Medical Aid for Palestinians (MAP), 'Two Healthcare Workers Killed Every Day on Average during Israel's Genocide in Gaza', Press Release, 7 October 2025, www.map.org.uk/latest/news/1772-two-healthcare-workers-killed-every-day-on-average-during-israelas-genocide-in-gaza/
43. Handicap International, 'Attacks on Healthcare', 5–6.
44. James Walker, 'Anger as Timeline Shows Israel's Repeated Gaza Ceasefire Breaches', *The National*, 5 December 2025, https://web.archive.org/web/20251208170312/https://www.thenational.scot/news/25673568.anger-timeline-shows-israels-repeated-gaza-ceasefire-breaches/; and Amnesty International, 'Israel/OPT: Post-Ceasefire: Israel's Genocide in the Occupied Gaza Strip Continues', 27 November 2025, 1–3, www.amnesty.org/en/documents/mde15/0527/2025/en/.
45. Amnesty International, 'Israel//OPT', 2–3.
46. Amy Walker and David Gritten, 'Israel to Bar 37 Aid Groups as UK and EU Warn of Severe Impact in Gaza', *BBC News*, 31 December 2025, www.bbc.com/news/articles/c1evp7weyv2o.
47. Médecins Sans Frontières, 'Gaza: Life in a Death Trap', 19 December 2024, 5, www.msf.org/life-death-trap-gaza-palestine; Physicians for Human Rights – Israel, 'Position Paper: Destruc-

tion of Conditions of Life: A Health Analysis of the Gaza Genocide', Reliefweb, July 2025, 11–12, https://reliefweb.int/report/occupied-palestinian-territory/position-paper-destruction-conditions-life-health-analysis-gaza-genocide; and Independent International Commission of Inquiry on the Occupied Palestinian Territory, including East Jerusalem, and Israel, 'Legal Analysis of the Conduct of Israel in Gaza Pursuant to the Convention on the Prevention and Punishment of the Crime of Genocide', UN Doc. A/HRC/60/CRP.3, 16 September 2025, 64, www.ohchr.org/sites/default/files/documents/hrbodies/hrcouncil/sessions-regular/session60/advance-version/a-hrc-60-crp-3.pdf.

48. Independent International Commission of Inquiry on the Occupied Palestinian Territory, including East Jerusalem, and Israel, 'Legal Analysis of the Conduct of Israel in Gaza', 47–48.

49. Amina Mukhtar, 'First, Do No Harm: In Defense as the Doctor as a Political Figure', *Law Beyond Borders*, Substack, 14 June 2025, https://substack.com/home/post/p-165910569.

50. Paul Blumenthal, 'Israeli President Suggests That Civilians in Gaza Are Legitimate Targets', *HuffPost*, 13 October 2023, www.huffingtonpost.co.uk/entry/israel-gaza-isaac-herzog_n_65295ee8e4b03ea0c004e2a8; and Independent International Commission of Inquiry on the Occupied Palestinian Territory, including East Jerusalem, and Israel, 'Detailed Findings on attacks carried out on and after 7 October 2023 in Israel', UN Doc. A/HRC/56/CRP.3, 54–59, www.ohchr.org/sites/default/files/documents/hrbodies/hrcouncil/sessions-regular/session56/a-hrc-56-crp-3.pdf.

51. United Nations, 'Gaza War: "Direct Hits" on More than 200 Schools Since Israeli Bombing Began', *UN News*, 27 March 2024, https://news.un.org/en/story/2024/03/1148031.

52. United Nations Office for the Coordination of Human-

itarian Affairs, 'Humanitarian Situation Update #179: Gaza Strip', 14 June 2024, www.ochaopt.org/content/humanitarian-situation-update-179-gaza-strip; and AJ Labs, 'Israel's Intensifying Attacks on Gaza Schools', *Al Jazeera*, 14 August 2024, www.aljazeera.com/news/2024/8/14/israels-intensifying-attacks-on-gaza-schools#:~:text=Almost%2085%20percent%20of%20school,have%20been%20damaged%20or%20destroyed.

53. European Training Foundation, 'Education and Training in the West Bank and Gaza: Facts and Figures', June 2025, 6, www.etf.europa.eu/sites/default/files/2025-07/Gaza%20update%202025%20final%2007 2025.pdf.

54. United Nations Office of the High Commissioner for Human Rights, 'UN Experts Deeply Concerned over "Scholasticide" in Gaza', 18 April 2024, www.ohchr.org/en/press-releases/2024/04/un-experts-deeply-concerned-over-scholasticide-gaza; and Islamic Relief, 'Gaza's Education Crisis', 17 February 2026, www.google.com/url?q=https://islamic-relief.org/news/gazas-education-crisis/&sa=D&source=docs&ust=1771419289333358&usg=AOvVawclhknEUZ84MWAw3dNnqY1k.

55. Nidal Al-Mughrabi, Simon Lewis and Suleiman Al-Khalidi, 'Arab Leaders Press Blinken for Gaza Ceasefire after School Blasts', *Reuters*, 4 November 2023, www.reuters.com/world/middle-east/us-arab-leaders-meet-over-gaza-palestinian-deaths-mount-2023-11-03/; and Meron Rapoport, 'Israeli Society's Dehumanization of Palestinians is Now Absolute', *+972 Magazine*, 23 August 2024, https://web.archive.org/web/20240825043602/https://www.972mag.com/dehumanization-moral-abyss-israelis/.

56. Sondos Fayoumi, 'Every University in Gaza Has Been Destroyed. So Have These Students' Dreams', *The Nation*, 26 July

2024, www.thenation.com/article/world/gaza-students-future/.
57. Ibtisam Mahdi, 'The Decimation of Gaza's Academia is "Impossible to Quantify"', *+972 Magazine*, 26 July 2024, www.972mag.com/gaza-academia-destruction-universities/.
58. Liam Stack and Bilal Shbair, 'With Schools in Ruins, Education in Gaza Will Be Hobbled for Years', *New York Times*, 6 May 2024, https://web.archive.org/web/20250206204657/https://www.nytimes.com/2024/05/06/world/middleeast/gaza-schools-damaged-destroyed.html.
59. Gaza People's Tribunal, 'Final Statement from the Jury of Conscience', 26 October 2025, 2, https://izu.edu.tr/docs/default-source/ciga-documents/final-gtj-statement.pdf; Chandni Desai, 'Israel Has Destroyed or Damaged 80% of Schools in Gaza. This is Scholasticide', *Guardian*, 8 June 2024, www.theguardian.com/commentisfree/article/2024/jun/08/israel-destroying-schools-scholasticide; and Gaza Academics and Administrators, 'Open Letter by Gaza Academics and University Administrators to the World', *Al Jazeera*, 29 May 2024, www.aljazeera.com/opinions/2024/5/29/open-letter-by-gaza-academics-and-university-administrators-to-the-world#:~:text=We%20call%20upon%20our%20friends,integrity%20of%20our%20academic%20institutions.
60. Wyre Davies, 'Gaza Destruction Risks Lost Generation of Children, Says UN Official', *BBC News*, 19 January 2024, www.bbc.co.uk/news/world-middle-east-68023080; Aric Toler, Sarah Kerr, Adam Sella, Arijeta Lajka and Chevaz Clarke, 'What Israeli Soldiers' Videos Reveal: Cheering Destruction and Mocking Gazans', *New York Times*, 6 February 2024, https://web.archive.org/web/20240725184618/https://www.nytimes.com/2024/02/06/world/middleeast/israel-idf-soldiers-war-social-media-video.html; and 'Israeli Soldiers Burn Al-Aqsa

University Library in Gaza Strip', *a news*, 24 May 2024, www.anews.com.tr/middle-east/2024/05/24/israeli-soldiers-burn-al-aqsa-university-library-in-gaza-strip.

61. 'Israel Blows Up Another University in Gaza', *Middle East Monitor*, 18 January 2024, www.middleeastmonitor.com/20240118-israels-military-occupies-and-destroys-israa-university-in-gaza/.

62. 'No University Left Standing in Gaza', *The Intercept*, 9 February 2024, https://theintercept.com/2024/02/09/deconstructed-gaza-university-education/.

63. Lemkin Institute for Genocide Prevention and Human Security, 'Statement on Why We Call the Israeli Attack on Gaza Genocide', 29 December 2023, www.lemkininstitute.com/statements-new-page/statement-on-why-we-call-the-israeli-attack-on-gaza-genocide.

64. Raphael Lemkin, *Axis Rule in Occupied Europe: Laws of Occupation – Analysis of Government – Proposals for Redress* (Carnegie Endowment for International Peace, 1944), 79–95.

65. Ernst Renan, 'What is a Nation?', from a lecture delivered at the Sorbonne, Paris, 11 March 1882, 'Qu'est-ce qu'une nation?', https://web.archive.org/web/20110827065548/http://www.cooper.edu/humanities/core/hss3/e_renan.html.

66. Committee to Protect Journalists, '2024 is Deadliest Year for Journalists in CPJ History; Almost 70% Killed by Israel', Special Report, 12 February 2025, cpj.org/special-reports/2024-is-deadliest-year-for-journalists-in-cpj-history-almost-70-percent-killed-by-israel/; and Nick Turse, 'News Graveyards: How Dangers to War Reporters Endanger the World', Costs of War, The Watson School of International and Public Affairs, 1 April 2025, https://costsofwar.watson.brown.edu/paper/news-graveyards-how-dangers-war-reporters-endanger-world.

67. Anthony Bellanger, 'Gaza Has Become Journalism's Graveyard. Killing Journalists is Killing the Truth', *Guardian*, 3 October 2025, www.theguardian.com/commentisfree/2025/oct/03/gaza-conflict-killing-journalists-has-become-journalism-graveyard.
68. Committee to Protect Journalists, 'Israel–Gaza War: Attacks on Journalists across the Region since October 7, 2023', https://cpj.org/issue/israel-gaza-war/.
69. International Federation of Journalists (IFJ), 'Israel: Two Years of Killing Journalists and Controlling the Narrative in Gaza', press release, 7 October 2025, www.ifj.org/media-centre/news/detail/category/press-releases/article/israel-two-years-of-killing-journalists-and-controlling-the-narrative-in-gaza.
70. Palestinian Centre for Human Rights, *Assassination of Truth: Killing of Journalists amid Genocide in Gaza*, n.d., https://pchrgaza.org/wp-content/uploads/2025/09/Journalists-Report-EN.pdf; United Nations Office at Geneva, 'Gaza: UNESCO Condemns "Unacceptable" Killing of Journalists', 12 August 2025, www.ungeneva.org/en/news-media/news/2025/08/109495/gaza-unesco-condemns-unacceptable-killing-journalists?utm_source=chatgpt.com.
71. William Christou and Emma Graham-Harrison, '"There Needs to Be Justice", UN Tells Israel after Gaza Hospital Bombing', *Guardian*, 26 August 2025, www.theguardian.com/world/2025/aug/26/un-demands-investigations-into-gaza-hospital-killings.
72. United Nations, 'OHCHR: There Can Be No Talk of a Free Press in the Occupied Palestinian Territory if Journalists Are Being Killed, and Threatened for Their Work', 2 May 2025, www.un.org/unispal/document/ohchr-there-can-be-no-talk-of-a-free-press-in-the-occupied-palestinian-territory-if-journalists-

are-being-killed-and-threatened-for-their-work/?utm_source=-chatgpt.com.

73. Extensive reporting on the famine is available, including: United Nations, 'Israel: Ban on 37 Aid Groups Makes Life Unbearable for Genocide Survivors in Palestine, Say UN Experts', 15 January 2026, www.un.org/unispal/document/israel-ban-on-37-aid-groups-makes-life-unbearable-for-genocide-survivors-in-palestine-say-un-experts/; United Nations Office for the Coordination of Humanitarian Affairs, 'Gaza Humanitarian Response: Situation Report No. 51', 19 December 2025, www.ochaopt.org/content/gaza-humanitarian-response-situation-report-no-51; Integrated Food Security, 'Gaza Strip: Famine Confirmed in Gaza Governorate, Projected to Expand', 22 August 2025, www.ipcinfo.org/ipcinfo-website/countries-in-focus-archive/issue-134/en/; Food and Agricultural Organization of the United Nations, 'UN Agencies Warn Key food and Nutrition Indicators Exceed Famine Thresholds in Gaza', 29 July 2025, www.fao.org/newsroom/detail/un-agencies-warn-key-food-and-nutrition-indicators-exceed-famine-thresholds-in-gaza/en?utm_source=chatgpt.com; and United Nations Office of the High Commissioner for Human Rights, 'Starvation and the Right to Food, with an Emphasis on the Palestinian People's Food Sovereignty', UN Doc. A/79/171, 17 July 2024, www.ohchr.org/en/documents/thematic-reports/a79171-starvation-and-right-food-emphasis-palestinian-peoples-food.

74. Forensic Architecture, '"No Traces of Life": Israel's Ecocide in Gaza 2023–2024', 29 March 2024, https://forensic-architecture.org/investigation/ecocide-in-gaza.

75. Fishermen's Union, Gaza Strip, 10 February 2024, www.facebook.com/photo?fbid=849046870566281&-set=a.438917454912560.

76. Neve Gordon and Muna Haddad, 'The Road to Famine', *New York Review*, 30 March 2024, www.nybooks.com/online/2024/03/30/the-road-to-famine-in-gaza/.
77. UNICEF, 'UN Agencies Warn Key Food and Nutrition Indicators Exceed Famine Thresholds in Gaza', 29 July 2025, www.unicef.org/press-releases/un-agencies-warn-key-food-and-nutrition-indicators-exceed-famine-thresholds-gaza.
78. World Health Organization, 'Famine Confirmed for First Time in Gaza', 22 August 2025, www.who.int/news/item/22-08-2025-famine-confirmed-for-first-time-in-gaza.
79. World Health Organization, 'Famine Confirmed'.
80. United Nations Office of the High Commissioner for Human Rights, 'Israel Must Stop Using Water as a Weapon of War: UN Expert', 17 November 2023, www.ohchr.org/en/press-releases/2023/11/israel-must-stop-using-water-weapon-war-un-expert.
81. United Nations Population Fund, 'Situation Report: Humanitarian Crisis in Palestine', 16 May 2025, Situation Report 17_April 2025.pdf.
82. Karen DeYoung and Cate Brown, 'Gaza Postwar Plan Envisions "Voluntary" Relocation of Entire Population', *Washington Post*, 2 September 2025, www.washingtonpost.com/national-security/2025/08/31/trump-gaza-plan-riviera-relocation/.

Chapter 4: Preventing genocide

83. *Bosnia* v *Serbia* [2007] ICJ Rep 43, para. 430 (capacity to influence and due diligence); and *South Africa* v *Israel*, Provisional Measures Order (26 January 2024); ICJ Advisory Opinion (19 July 2024).
84. International Law Commission, *Articles on Responsibility of*

States for Internationally Wrongful Acts (2001) ('ARSIWA'), arts 2–4.

85. *Barcelona Traction, Light and Power Company, Limited* (*Belgium* v *Spain*) (Second Phase) [1970] ICJ Rep 3, paras. 33–34.

86. Geneva Convention (I) for the Amelioration of the Condition of the Wounded and Sick in Armed Forces in the Field (adopted 12 August 1949, entered into force 21 October 1950) 75 UNTS 31, Common art 1.

87. Convention on the Prevention and Punishment of the Crime of Genocide (adopted 9 December 1948, entered into force 12 January 1951) 78 UNTS 277, art I.

88. Rome Statute of the International Criminal Court (adopted 17 July 1998, entered into force 1 July 2002) 2187 UNTS 90, arts. 86–89.

89. International Law Commission, 'Draft Articles on Responsibility of States for Internationally Wrongful Acts, with commentaries, in Report of the International Law Commission on the Work of its Fifty-Third Session', United Nations General Assembly Records, 56th Sess., Supp. No. 10, at 43, UN Doc. A/56/10 (2001) Annex to GA Res. 56/83 (12 December 2001) (hereinafter ARSIWA).

90. Application of the Convention on the Prevention and Punishment of the Crime of Genocide (*South Africa* v *Israel*), Order of 26 January 2024 (Provisional Measures), paras. 54–74, 78–86.

91. Irene Pietropaoli, 'Obligations of Third States and Corporations to Prevent and Punish Genocide in Gaza', 5 June 2024, www.somo.nl/wp-content/uploads/2024/06/Obligations-of-Third-States-and-Corporations-to-Prevent-and-Punish-Genocide-in-Gaza-3.pdf.

92. International Court of Justice, 'Legal Consequences arising

from the Policies and Practices of Israel in the Occupied Palestinian Territory, including East Jerusalem', Advisory Opinion, 19 July 2024, paras 260–278 (hereinafter Advisory Opinion of July 2024).

93. ICJ, Advisory Opinion of July 2024, para. 267 (emphasis added).

94. ARSIWA, paras. 273–277; International Law Commission, 'Report of the International Law Commission on the Work of Its Fifty-Third Session', United Nations General Assembly Official Records, 56th sess, Supp No 10, UN Doc A/56/10 (23 April–1 June and 2 July–10 August 2001) ch. IV(E)(1) ('Draft Articles on State Responsibility for Internationally Wrongful Acts') arts. 40–1; *Legal Consequences of the Construction of a Wall* (n 4) 200 [159].

95. This section has been cited frequently in subsequent statements by states, organisations and institutions endorsing the ICJ's decision. For example, the Hague Group, which is a coalition of Global South states dedicated to taking collective action in support of Palestinian rights as articulated by international law, has referenced the *Opinion* in support of its decision to suspend arms transfers to Israel. The Hague Group, 'Inaugural Joint Statement', 31 January 2025, https://thehaguegroup.org/meetings-hague-en.

96. Advisory Opinion of July 2024, para. 278

97. Francesca Albanese, '*From Economy of Occupation to Economy of Genocide: Report of the Special Rapporteur on the Situation of Human Rights in the Palestinian Territories Occupied Since 1967*', UN Doc. A/HRC/59/23, 2 July 2025, www.ohchr.org/en/documents/country-reports/ahrc5923-economy-occupation-economy-genocide-report-special-rapporteur.

98. Human Rights Council, 'Human Rights Situation', UN

Doc. A/HRC/RES/55/28, 16 April 2024, para.14.
99. *Arms Trade Treaty*, 2 April 2013, entered into force 24 December 2014, 3013 UNTS 269, arts. 6–7; ARSIWA, art. 16.
100. UK Government, 'Overseas Security and Justice Assistance (OSJA): Human Rights Guidance', 2017: 4, https://assets.publishing.service.gov.uk/media/5a81781be5274a2e87dbdcco/OSJA_Guidance_2017.pdf.
101. Who Profits, *Financing Land Grab: The Direct Involvement of Israeli Banks in the Israeli Settlement Enterprise*, February 2017, www.whoprofits.org/writable/uploads/publications/1668630886_81fd6b82b80761f6a853.pdf.
102. *Legal Consequences Arising from the Policies and Practices of Israel in the Occupied Palestinian Territory, including East Jerusalem*, Advisory Opinion, 19 July 2024, para. 278 (duty to abstain from economic relations and to prevent private actor support).
103. International Court of Justice, *Legal Consequences for States of the Continued Presence of South Africa in Namibia (South West Africa) notwithstanding Security Council Resolution 276* (1970) (Advisory Opinion) [1971] Rep 16; International Court of Justice, Legal 'Consequences of the Construction of a Wall in the Occupied Palestinian Territory (Advisory Opinion)' [2004] Rep 136, para. 159; and ICJ Advisory Opinion (19 July 2024), paras. 273–278.
104. Jinan Bastaki, 'The "Capacity to Influence", State Responsibility, and the Obligation to Prevent Genocide', *Opinio Juris*, 30 March 2024, https://opiniojuris.org/2024/03/30/the-capacity-to-influence-state-responsibility-and-the-obligation-to-prevent-genocide/.
105. Protocol Additional to the Geneva Conventions of 12 August 1949, and Relating to the Protection of Victims of International Armed Conflicts (Protocol I), 8 June 1977, 1125

U.N.T.S. 3, arts. 54 and 70; and Jean-Marie Henckaerts and Louise Doswald-Beck, eds., *Customary International Humanitarian Law, Vol. 1: Rules* (Cambridge: Cambridge University Press, 2005).

106. International Court of Justice, Advisory Opinion of 22 October 2025: Obligations of Israel in Relation to the Presence and Activities of the United Nations, Other International Organizations and Third States in and in Relation to the Occupied Palestinian Territory.

107. Convention on the Prevention and Punishment of the Crime of Genocide, Art. II(c), 9 December 1948, 78 U.N.T.S. 277, 280 (deliberately inflicting conditions of life calculated to bring about physical destruction).

108. Rome Statute of the International Criminal Court, arts. 86–89, 17 July 1998, 2187 U.N.T.S. 3, arts. 86–89 (cooperation); art. 27 (irrelevance of official capacity) and related jurisprudence on immunities under the Statute.

109. Charter of the International Military Tribunal (Nuremberg), annexed to the Agreement for the Prosecution and Punishment of the Major War Criminals of the European Axis ('London Agreement') of 8 August 1945, 82 U.N.T.S. 279 and Trial of the Major War Criminals Before the International Military Tribunal (IMT) (1947), vol. 1, 223–224 (individual responsibility principle).

110. Rome Statute, arts. 6 (genocide), 25(3)(c) (aiding and abetting/assistance) and 25(3)(e) (direct and public incitement); Elements of Crimes, ICC-ASP/1/3 (2002).

111. Rome Statute, art. 28(b) (superior responsibility for civilian superiors); and ICC jurisprudence on 'effective control' and 'necessary and reasonable measures' (e.g. Bemba Appeal Judgement, ICC-01/05-01/08-3636).

Chapter 6: Complicity in genocide

112. Transcript from Prime Minister Keir Starmer's address to British troops at RAF Akrotiri, Cyprus, 10 December 2024, www.gov.uk/government/speeches/pms-address-to-british-troops-in-raf-akrotiri-cyprus-10-december-2024.
113. These figures refer to the value of UK exports to Israel specifically as part of the F-35 programme. CAAT reached these figures by combining 1) the estimated value of the 15 per cent of parts made in the UK for each plane delivered since 7 October 2023 with 2) the rate of spare part transfer.
114. Campaign Against Arms Trade, 'Government Exempts F-35 from Export Licence Suspension – On Same Day Evidence Emerges Israel Used It in Attack on Gaza "Safe Zone"', 2 September 2024, https://caat.org.uk/news/investigation-reveals-israel-used-partly-uk-made-f-35-in-attack-on-gaza-humanitarian-zone-in-july-killing-90/; and Danwatch, 'Major Civilian Casualties: Danish-equipped Fighter Jets behind Bloody Attack in Gaza', 1 September 2024, https://danwatch.dk/en/major-civilian-casualties-danish-equipped-fighter-jets-behind-bloody-attack-in-gaza/.
115. Palestinian Youth Movement, Workers for a Free Palestine, Progressive International, 'Exposing UK Arms Exports to Israel', 7 May 2025, https://static1.squarespace.com/static/664aed65d320123f2b3ab647/t/681b13a2197d634a11d746c0/1746604963269/Report-ExposingUKArmsExportsToIsrael-05072025.pdf.
116. Palestinian Youth Movement, Workers for a Free Palestine, Progressive International, 'Exposing UK Arms Exports to Israel', 1.
117. John McEvoy, 'Fighter Jet Parts Sent Through UK Airport to Israel', *Declassified UK*, 18 June 2025, www.declassifieduk.

org/fighter-jet-parts-sent-through-uk-airport-to-israel/.
118. Matt Kennard and Abdullah Farooq, 'Gaza Spy Flights From UK Base On Cyprus Secretly Shift to Plane Leased by Company with Billions in US Military Contracts', *Internationalist 360*, 4 August 2025, https://libya360.wordpress.com/2025/08/04/gaza-spy-flights-from-uk-base-on-cyprus-secretly-shift-to-plane-leased-by-company-with-billions-in-us-military-contracts/.
119. Matt Kennard, 'The British Spy Squad Assisting Israel as It Bombs Gaza', *Declassified UK*, 11 June 2024, www.declassifieduk.org/the-british-spy-squad-assisting-israel-as-it-bombs-gaza/.
120. Matt Kennard, 'Britain Secretly Sent 500 Extra Troops to Cyprus Base Being Used to Supply Weapons to Israel', *Declassified UK*, 12 December 2023, www.declassifieduk.org/britain-secretly-sent-500-extra-troops-to-cyprus-base-being-used-to-supply-weapons-to-israel/.
121. Written questions, answers and statements, UK Parliament, 'Israel: Armed Forces – Question for Ministry of Defence', UIN 12736, tabled on 1 February 2024, https://questions-statements.parliament.uk/written-questions/detail/2024-02-01/12736.
122. Written questions, answers and statements, UK Parliament, 'Israel: Military Aid – Question for Ministry of Defence', UIN 56822, tabled on 3 June 2025, https://questions-statements.parliament.uk/written-questions/detail/2025-06-03/56822.
123. Patrick Wintour, 'UK Accused of "Garbled Messaging" as Trade Envoy Visits Israel to Boost Links', *Guardian*, 28 May 2025, www.theguardian.com/politics/2025/may/28/uk-trade-envoy-lord-austin-visit-israel-talks-suspended-sparks-criticism.

124. MEE Staff, 'Israel–Palestine War: Keir Starmer Supports Israel's "Right" to Cut Gaza's Water and Power', *Middle East Eye*, 11 October 2023, www.middleeasteye.net/news/israel-palestine-war-keir-starmer-criticised-right-cut-gaza-water-power.
125. Parallel Parliament, 'Israel and Gaza: Rishi Sunak Excerpts', 16 October 2023, https://parallelparliament.co.uk/mp/rishi-sunak/debate/2023-10-16/commons/commons-chamber/israel-and-gaza.
126. International Court of Justice, 'Legal Consequences Arising from the Policies and Practices of Israel in the Occupied Palestinian Territory, including East Jerusalem', 20 July 2023, para. 5, www.icj-cij.org/sites/default/files/case-related/186/186-20230725-wri-15-00-en.pdf.
127. United Nations Office of the High Commissioner for Human Rights, 'UN Experts Urge United Kingdom Not to Misuse Terrorism Laws against Protest Group Palestine Action', 1 July 2025, www.ohchr.org/en/press-releases/2025/07/un-experts-urge-united-kingdom-not-misuse-terrorism-laws-against-protest.
128. Dominic Casciani, 'Palestine Action Ban Ruled Unlawful but Group Remains Proscribed for Now', *BBC News*, 13 February 2026, www.bbc.co.uk/news/articles/c3wleezq73no.
129. United Nations Association, Coventry Branch, '310 Civil Servants "Longstanding Concern" with UK Gaza Policy', 10 June 2025, https://unacov.uk/310-civil-servants-longstanding-concern-with-uk-gaza-policy/.
130. Middle East Eye, 'What Happened to the Boy Who Saw His Grandmother Killed While Waving a White Flag?', 6 October 2024, www.middleeasteye.net/live-blog/live-blog-update/what-happened-boy-who-saw-his-grandmother-killed-while-waving-white-flag; Euro-Med Human Rights Monitor,

'Israel's Execution of Three Palestinians – One of Whom was Injured – in Hospital is a Double Crime', 30 January 2024, https://euromedmonitor.org/en/article/6129; and Reuters, 'Bakeries Smashed in Israel Bombardment Key to Gaza Hunger Crisis', 28 February 2024, www.reuters.com/world/middle-east/bakeries-smashed-israel-bombardment-key-gaza-hunger-crisis-2024-02-28/.

131. Patrick Wintour, 'No Evidence of Genocide in Gaza, UK Lawyers Say in Arms Export Case', *Guardian*, 13 May 2025, www.theguardian.com/world/2025/may/13/no-evidence-of-genocide-in-gaza-uk-lawyers-say-in-arms-export-case.

132. Middle East Eye, 'UK Assessed There was "No Serious Risk" of Israel Committing Genocide in Gaza', 13 May 2025, www.middleeasteye.net/news/uk-assessed-there-was-no-serious-risk-israel-committing-genocide-gaza.

133. Sky News, 'Lammy: Does the UK Think There's a Genocide in Gaza?', 9 September 2025, https://news.sky.com/video/lammy-does-the-uk-think-theres-a-genocide-in-gaza-13427827.

Conclusion: The Gaza Doctrine

134. Jonathan Whittall, 'Destroy, Displace, Dismantle: Israel's Gaza Doctrine Comes to Lebanon', *Al Jazeera*, 13 March 2026, www.aljazeera.com/opinions/2026/3/13/destroy-displace-dismantle-israels-gaza-doctrine-comes-to-lebanon.

135. WHO, 'Conflict Deepens Health Crisis across Middle East, WHO Says', 11 March 2026, www.who.int/news/item/11-03-2026-conflict-deepens-health-crisis-across-middle-east--who-says.

136. William Christou and Abbas Abdelkarim, 'Israel Delib-

erately Targeting Medical Facilities in Southern Lebanon, Say Health Workers', *Guardian*, 21 March 2026, www.theguardian.com/world/2026/mar/21/israel-targeting-medical-facilities-south-lebanon-health-workers.

137. Talha Burki, 'Destruction of Gaza's Only Cancer Specialist Hospital', *The Lancet Oncology* 26, no. 5 (May 2025), www.thelancet.com/journals/lanonc/article/PIIS1470-2045(25)00192-5/fulltext?rss=yes.

138. (22) روپنامرک نیسح Hossein.Kermanpour on X: 'Eight days of war have brought devastation to civilians in Iran. • Over 10,000 civilians injured • More than 1,200 killed (martyrs) • 200 children under 12 among the dead (martyrs) • Around 200 women killed (martyrs) • About 1,400 women injured Healthcare infrastructure', X, 8 March 2026, https://x.com/HKermanpour/status/2030548540229873999.

139. Opinion, 'Finding Fault for the Deadly U.S. Strike on a School in Iran', *New York Times*, 12 March 2026, www.nytimes.com/2026/03/12/opinion/us-iran-school-missle-strike.html.

140. Benjamin Netanyahu, 'PM Netanyahu's Remarks at his Press Conference', Prime Minister's Office, 12 March 2026, www.gov.il/en/pages/spoke-ari-press120326.